I0128628

THE PURSUIT OF
THE POWER-SUIT

Yasmina Nessim

THE PURSUIT OF
THE POWER-SUIT

Optimising Women's
Wellbeing Today Through
the Application of Science
to Style

Fashion and Personal Style Studies

Collection Editor

Joseph H. Hancock II

First published in 2025 by Lived Places Publishing

All rights reserved. No part of this publication may be reproduced, stored in a retrieval system, or transmitted in any form or by any means, electronic, mechanical, photocopying, recording, or otherwise, without prior permission in writing from the publisher.

No part of this book may be used or reproduced in any manner for the purpose of training artificial intelligence technologies or systems. In accordance with Article 4(3) of the Digital Single Market Directive 2019/790, Lived Places Publishing expressly reserves this work from the text and data mining exception.

The author and editor have made every effort to ensure the accuracy of the information contained in this publication but assume no responsibility for any errors, inaccuracies, inconsistencies, or omissions. Likewise, every effort has been made to contact copyright holders. If any copyright material has been reproduced unwittingly and without permission, the publisher will gladly receive information enabling them to rectify any error or omission in subsequent editions.

Copyright © 2025 Lived Places Publishing

British Library Cataloguing in Publication Data
A CIP record for this book is available from the British Library.

ISBN: 9781916704763 (pbk)
ISBN: 9781916704787 (ePDF)
ISBN: 9781916704770 (ePUB)

The right of Yasmina Nessim to be identified as the Author of this work has been asserted by them in accordance with the Copyright, Design and Patents Act 1988.

Cover design by Fiachra McCarthy
Book design by Rachel Trolove of Twin Trail Design
Typeset by Newgen Publishing, UK

Lived Places Publishing
P.O. Box 1845
47 Echo Avenue
Miller Place, NY 11764

www.livedplacespublishing.com

Abstract

The pursuit of the power-suit explores the transformative intersection of fashion and psychology to optimise women's wellbeing in contemporary society. Drawing from both academic theory and lived experiences, the book presents a new framework – Yasmina's very own SUITS™ – that outlines five pillars of fashion-driven wellness: Self-Expression, Understanding the Body, Identifying and Illustrating Our Emotions, Targeting Goals, and Social Unity. With a narrative that blends research with storytelling, it offers readers both the science and soul behind personal style, empowering them to use clothing as a strategic tool for confidence, identity, and mental health. It is both a call to curiosity and a manifesto for self-reclamation – reminding women everywhere that sometimes, the most powerful transformations begin in the fabric of intention.

Key words

Fashion psychology; wellbeing; identity; self-expression; positive psychology; clothing and mental health; body image. emotional regulation; enclothed cognition; social belonging; personal style; self-perception theory; fashion and personality

Acknowledgements

Yes, this is a book. A tangible object with over 45,000 words stitched across its pages, but even still, there will never be enough words, or the right ones, to fully express the gratitude I feel for those who helped bring it into being. This section may be printed in ink, but know that each sentence is written in awe, reverence, and the most profound of thanks.

To David and the LPP family: thank you for believing in what I had to say, and more importantly, how I wanted to say it. For letting me chase my moonshot long before I expected to even reach orbit. To my editor, Joe, your patience, encouragement, and ideas brought not just structure, but sanity. You have both held space for my pace, my health, and my voice, and for that alone, this book owes you more than I could ever repay.

To my mentor and enduring North Star, Aurore Bardey – this book quite simply would not exist without you. You offered me your wisdom when the world offered doubt. You gave me resources and resilience, both. In a sea of sceptics, you were my lighthouse. This is, and will always be, for you.

To my clients – the brave, brilliant souls who entrusted me with their stories and allowed me to carry them into the light. Thank you for your faith, your vulnerability, and your grace. Your courage shaped these pages, and your compassion gave them purpose. I am forever indebted. And to my right hand, Yasmin – the quiet powerhouse behind the curtain – you carried the weight of a business so I could carry the weight of this manuscript. May the world someday know the marvel you are. You are irreplaceable and I am forever grateful that you, in essence, are the pstyled family.

To my sisters, best friends, and tireless inner circle – my beloved panel of patient, sleepless, over-polled guinea pigs. You read, re-read, listened, nodded, questioned, affirmed, and fed me – both emotionally and, occasionally, literally. I love you more than prose can hold. Free copies are coming, as promised.

To my parents and siblings – who applauded this dream when it was still a conversation at a local coffee shop, or a dream on a walk. You saw the seedling before there was a forest. I owe every word, every chapter, every page to your belief in me. I am who I am because of you.

And finally – most monumentally – to my husband. My anchor, my home, my greatest collaborator in life and leftovers. For two years, you have held me up when I had nothing left, ushered me to bed when I forgot time existed, fed me when I wouldn't feed myself, and carried the emotional weight of this project with the kind of grace only you possess. You believed in this book even when I didn't. And more astonishingly – you believed in me. I love you endlessly.

To you, dear reader, whether you purchased this book, borrowed it, stumbled upon it in passing, or read just a single page – thank you. You are the lifeblood of this mission, the reason this work can ripple beyond me. Thank you for caring about fashion and feeling, for choosing to reflect and grow. In doing so, you carry the message forward that clothing can heal, that stories matter, and that style, when wielded with intention, is nothing short of revolutionary.

Thank you – all of you – for everything.

Contents

Learning objectives

By the end of this book, readers will be able to:

1. Define fashion psychology and understand its relevance to mental health and wellbeing
2. Identify and apply the SUITS™ framework to enhance personal style and psychological wellness
3. Reflect on the emotional, cognitive, and social impacts of their clothing choices
4. Use fashion as a method for self-discovery, emotional regulation, and goal-setting
5. Recognise the historical and cultural dimensions of dress and their psychological implications
6. Evaluate the psychological effects of intentional versus unintentional outfit choices
7. Reframe personal style as a strategic and empowering wellness practice

1
Introduction

"In the masque we may clothe our fantasies, moods and aspirations, the angel, devil, butterfly and flower within us each having its brief hour."

– Silvia Bliss (1916)

All fashion enthusiasts are well aware of the radical volatility and overwhelming catalogue of brand and clothing options that the fashion arena suffers from. If you too have been blessed with the intolerable pain of falling madly and erratically in love – I'm talking head-over-red-sole-heels in love – with all things fashion, then you too will know that the chaos and utter madness of the *monde de la mode* is completely worth it. All individuals associated with the fashion world – be they industry conglomerates, stylists, designers, or even devout shoppers – will preach their belief in the symbolic values and mystical powers of their clothing, unintentionally revealing the sheer force that garments have on their psyche and emotionality. Making all those unbearable moments of fashion anxiety, or any form of anxiety, really, truly invaluable. Speaking of anxiety and all its irritable forms, welcome, one and all, to the undeniable and underestimated world of fashion psychology.

Given that the phenomenon of fashion psychology is fairly young in its nature, there are a myriad of 'definitions' and 'interpretations' dancing between the worlds of academia and the blogosphere. What's more, for what may seem like an eternity, fashion in its entirety was presented negatively, if at all, within the realm of contemporary psychology. It wasn't until recently that a handful of [fashion] psychologists, myself included, helped breathe new life into the significant number of positive and enlightening associations involved within the art and science of fashion and dress. Our research has exposed the truly unjust treatment of fashion within psychology, which has continuously disregarded the union between individual clothing practices and intrapsychic experiences (Masuch & Hefferon, 2014). My research in particular is unique in its exploration of fashion choices from a positive psychological perspective, and focuses predominantly on wellbeing and the physiological rapport between individuals and their clothes. My definition of fashion psychology, therefore, involves the ways in which the fashion industry, clothing, and fashion in all its forms impact our mental health and psychological wellbeing. Fashion psychology is, quite simply, understanding how fashion choices can mould and manipulate the human mind.

To all the haters and naysayers who roll their eyes at the mere thought of fashion having such immense power over the human psyche, I see you and I say this: you, my darling, are already a part and product of the wonderful world of fashion. Your daily ritual of getting dressed, as apathetic as it may be. Your almost ceremonial peek in the storefront window on your daily commute, your inevitable shopping haul on your I'm-not-shopping-on-this-vacation vacation, and above all else, the love and comfort you shamelessly feel in that great, grey sweater are all indicators that you, yes you, are part of the universal fabric of fashion. While you come to terms with your raw and newfound appreciation for fashion, allow me to help you not only embrace it but, better yet, use it to your utmost advantage.

The fundamental purpose of my work is to help people from across the globe understand and apply fashion psychology in the context of mental health. It is dedicated to providing individuals with an ignored and yet inescapable vehicle for enhancing their wellbeing. After years of academic, scientific, empirical, and practical research, my work has proven that the application of fashion psychology in one's daily ritual can maximise their wellbeing in ways that are truly and tear-jerkingly amazing. And all it takes is a suit. Or should I say, S.U.I.T.S.:

Self-Expression; Understanding the Body; Identifying and Illustrating Our Emotions; Targeting Goals; and Social Unity.

Oh, the power that that one suit holds.

S.U.I.T.S. is my fashion psychology formula to help anyone and everyone optimise their wellbeing through outfit curation and fashion choices. The formula is based on compound research and mechanisms, all of which are thought to be decisive hallmarks of wellbeing (Hefferon & Boniwell, 2011). Centuries of analyses have shown that projects and elements that influence happiness are based on their impact and ability to facilitate self-expression (Christiansen, 2000), the first and most unmistakable component. The identity-establishing and expressive powers of fashion have been an invariable topic for decades, with a consensus that clothing choices play a pivotal role in identity formation and identity management (Bernard, 1996). Similarly, the second component is based on the love, appreciation, and understanding of the body. It is dedicated to the celebration of a healthy and respectful internal narrative of one's physical assets. Contrary to the invasive and unwelcome notions made by popular media sources, positive body perception is argued to be associated with subjective happiness (Swami et al., 2010) and wellbeing (Tiggemann et al., 2009). Identifying and illustrating our emotions is anchored in the management and manipulation of our feelings through introspection and reflection. It is based on the premise that fashion choices can be employed as a coping mechanism to regulate mood; argued to be one of the fundamental indicators of emotional intelligence and wellbeing (Goleman, 1996).

Targeting goals. Pretty self-explanatory. But it is less concerned with the mere act of ticking tasks off an endless to-do list, and more to do with how garment association and assignment can help individuals achieve their goals, regardless of what they may be. Personal or professional, big or small, people build meaning in life through goal pursuits (Emmons, 1999). And finally, saving the best and most heartwarming for last: the act of social unity. Self-expression's little sister, but equally as brilliant. A relationship built up of two coexisting yet contradictory psychological motivations: differentiation and imitation (Simmel, 1957 [1905]). The natural human desire to be unique and individualistic, whilst in parallel serving the innate need to belong. Creating a sense of community, feeling safe and seen in an environment complete with like-minded people, and knowing that in this vast and fast-paced world you are truly never alone, is the foundation for true and everlasting wellbeing. Our clothes, something as simple as a t-shirt, have the ability to communicate volumes of nonverbal words to those around us, which in turn might trigger a smile, a curious sideways glance, or even a nod of appreciation from a stranger who just might become a friend. A friend, and a bond, and a connection. And a it took was a t-shirt.

There's an undeniable rise in mental health concerns worldwide, with an approximate 13% increase in conditions and disorders over the last decade. Complications related to mental health and wellness now cause 1 in 5 years lived with disability, with a substantial effect on all areas of life: from professional and academic performance, to the sustenance and development of relationships, and even one's ability to participate in the community.

With that rise, however, comes a majestic boom in the need for and search for a global and uninhibited discussion on mental health and wellbeing, including, but not limited to, topics such as anxiety, depression, and emotional stability. The fundamental purpose of this book – and my very reason for being – is to aid in the recognition and education of mental health and wellbeing, in the hope that we may collaboratively and collectively develop significant and accessible solutions to these issues. More specifically, the intention of this book is to help people everywhere understand how fashion, in its magnitude, can contribute to the improvement of mental health and overall wellbeing. The chapters that follow are not limited to the elaboration of the theory and science behind the five pillars of wellbeing, but also include the sincere and unfiltered stories of individuals who have incorporated fashion psychology into their lives. The stories in this book have monumentally helped make sense of an extraordinary topic that, until recent years, had not been looked at with the scientific and professional rigour that it deserves and demands, that humans around the planet need, and that has been disre-garded as an afterthought. And above all else, the stories in this book perfectly illustrate that, when achieved, even just a little bit, happiness really is attainable and it is truly gorgeous: a majestic symphony of calm and confidence with fashion in the role of conductor.

2
Well-dressed and wellbeing: A history

It began, as most things do, with a leaf. A humble fig leaf, plucked not for its verdant beauty but for its modesty, making humanity's first foray into fashion. From that moment onward, clothing ceased to be merely functional. It became symbolic – a statement, a shield, a canvas. And with that evolution came the most fascinating and complex question of all: why do we dress the way we do? The history of fashion psychology is not stitched together by hemlines and trends alone; it is a living, breathing testament to the human condition – to our vanity, our vulnerability, and our deeply ingrained need for self-expression. For millennia, we have slipped into garments to cover our flesh, yes, but also, and perhaps more importantly, to craft identity, to signal status, to seduce, and, if the mood strikes, to deceive. So, welcome, reader, to a brief but mind-blowing history of fashion, in a way, perhaps, that you may not have thought of it before.

In its infancy, fashion was survival. Furs and hides shielded Palaeolithic bodies from the elements, while rudimentary adornments marked tribal identity. Archaeological evidence shows that as early as 20,000 years ago, humans were already using dress as a form of storytelling: a bone-carved Venus figurine found in France, for instance, depicts a woman draped in a twisted-fibre skirt – the first known garment of its kind (Barber, 1994). Across continents, petroglyphs – stone carvings created by ancient peoples – etched the first known "runways", immortalising what they wore and how they lived. Honestly, if that's not the most exclusive debut issue of a fashion magazine, I, quite frankly, don't know what is. Now, fast forward several millennia, and dress became not just a reflection of culture but a tool for it. The Egyptians draped themselves in linen to reflect purity and divine power. The Greeks elevated drapery into sculpture, their flowing chitons and ode to aesthetic perfection. Meanwhile, the Romans – those master propagandists – used dress as a political billboard. The toga, once a symbol of Roman citizenship, became a sartorial shorthand for power, class, and masculinity. Fashion was no longer about survival; it was about the narrative.

The true pivot towards fashion psychology began when scholars realised that clothing was, in truth, a language. Sociologist Georg Simmel (1904) first described fashion as the "social skin", a surface upon which individuals projected their place in the hierarchy. This was a dance of imitation and distinction – people seeking both to conform and to stand out. The paradox of fashion, Simmel argued, was that it offered a means to express individuality whilst simultaneously enforcing conformity. By the twentieth century, psychologists took the stage. Yay! Ernst Dichter, the pioneering consumer psychologist, declared that "clothing is packaging", a psychological wrapper for the self (Dichter, 1964). His research revealed that fashion was, at the very least, aesthetic, and at the very best, medicinal. During times of recession, for instance, people dressed brightly, seeking chromatic antidotes to economic gloom. Clothing, he found, was aspirational, hopeful, and optimistic. It allowed the wearer to slip into a version of themselves that felt more powerful, more beautiful, and more alive. In 1928, Paul Nystrom, one of the earliest theorists of consumer behaviour, wrote that fashion was "the prevailing style at any given time" (Nystrom, 1928). And by 1958, psychologist Dwight Robinson argued that it was far more insidious: a relentless "pursuit of novelty for its own sake" (Robinson, 1958). Ah, the sceptics. But fashion, they'd eventually realise, was an addictive elixir of self-reinvention. One dress could rejuvenate, and another silhouette could offer the illusion of rebirth. It was extraordinary.

By the latter half of the century, the field began to take on its modern shape. The 1960s brought with them an age of rebellion: miniskirts, leather jackets, and free love. Fashion became a megaphone for politics, sexuality, and identity. It was no coincidence that psychologists turned their gaze to the wardrobe. George B. Sproles (1979) formalised the psychological models of fashion behaviour, identifying diverse motivations for sartorial choices: escapism, creativity, rebellion, conformity, and status signalling. His contemporaries, William Gorden and Dominic Infante, argued that fashion was a form of communication (Gorden & Infante, 1987), a "body idiom" akin to non-verbal language (Knapp, 1972). And by the 1980s, Solomon's *Psychology of Fashion* (1985) declared the field a legitimate area of study – double yay – blending consumer behaviour with social identity theory. His work underscored the fundamental truth: fashion was not simply a response to trends; it was a mirror to the soul. Let's all take a collective breath, reader, because that was the moment fashion psychology stopped lurking in the dressing room and officially took centre stage.

And we're back.

At its core, fashion psychology was revealed to be a study of dualities – ego and insecurity, beauty and decay, individuality and conformity. It showed that people dressed not just to express who they were but who they longed to be. Clothing became a talisman for self-belief. And with that, throughout the 1990s and early 2000s, researchers such as Sharon Lennon and Leslie Davis expanded on these theories, exploring how clothing influences self-esteem, body image, and emotional wellbeing (Lennon & Davis, 1989). Their work found that clothing could alter mood and cognition, turning the wardrobe into a form of cognitive therapy. Adam and Galinsky (2012) later coined terms like *enclothed cognition* – the phenomenon where what you wear influences how you think and behave. And just like that, the science was in. Today, fashion psychology is both an academic field and a cultural force. It informs marketing strategies, consumer behaviour, and even therapy – *hello*. It reveals that the little black dress is more than a closet staple; it's an armour and an immensely powerful tool to help treat anxiety. That jeans are not just everyday casualwear; they are emotional barometers and occasionally a silent cry for help. The science has spoken – and continues to speak, louder than a runway finale – our clothes may be a mirror, yes, but they're also a chisel, carving out the edges of who we are yet to become. And so, as you hold this book, dear reader, remember that fashion is far more than fabric; it is history, psychology, rebellion, and redemption. It is a language we all speak, whether we intend to or not. As with any new language, fluency starts with the basics. So, consider this your glossary, your very own sartorial Rosetta Stone.

Key definitions to help in the pursuit

Like any language, the world of fashion psychology comes with its own lexicon – a glossary of terms that define the subtle, yet powerful, ways clothing and the human mind intertwine. Here's your primer, reader, to help you grasp what's to come.

Dress vs. clothing vs. costume

Let's start with the basics, shall we? While these terms are often used interchangeably, they each carry distinct meanings in fashion psychology. *Dress* refers to the full assemblage of body modifications and supplements. This includes not just garments but also hairstyles, makeup, tattoos, and even scent, a complete sensory presentation of the self (Eicher & Roach-Higgins, 1992). *Clothing,* on the other hand, is more specific. It refers exclusively to the fabric enclosures that cover the body. Unlike dress, it omits other modifications, and inevitably introduces personal or social values: i.e. covering is good, and revealing is bad – at least, according to certain puritanical codes of dress. *Costume*, meanwhile, denotes attire reserved for specific social roles or activities. It is "out-of-everyday" dress – what one might wear to a masquerade ball, a historical reenactment, or perhaps a *really* eccentric Monday meeting. Together, these terms form the foundation of how we describe what we wear and how we wear it. But for the sake of simplicity – and because we have no interest in being fashionably outdated – consider them interchangeable in this book. After all, who are we to declare what is costume and what is couture? What is good taste and what is simply good fun? The above distinctions are for your future trivia nights, dear reader, for the purposes of this book, it's all just fashion. Glorious, expressive, limitless fashion.

Appearance vs. dress

In the great Venn diagram of fashion psychology, dress and appearance overlap, but they are not one and the same. *Appearance* is the broader of the two; it encompasses not only dress but also the undressed body – including shape, skin tone, and even the fleeting language of gesture and expression. *Dress*, in contrast, is narrower, focusing solely on the external modifications and adornments we apply to the body. Think of it this way: appearance is the whole visual novel, while dress is the cover art, the carefully curated first impression.

The functions of dress

Since the early twentieth century, scholars have identified distinct functions of dress – each one a psychological puzzle piece contributing to the larger picture of why we wear what we wear. *Physical protection* is, quite literally, dress that shields us from the elements – faux-fur-lined coats for frost and linen shirts for sun. *Psychological protection,* on the other hand, refers to the moments when, sometimes, the armour is metaphorical. A tailored power suit becomes a shield against impostor syndrome. A leather jacket becomes a cloak of confidence. *Modesty* refers to the age-old social construct of covering the body for the sake of decorum. *Attraction* is dress as flirtation, a visual language of allure. The short sundress. The sharp tuxedo. The just-right amount of décolletage. *Status signalling* refers to clothing as currency – the monogrammed handbag and red-bottom heels that might as well come with a portable spotlight and string quartet. *Adornment* is in reference to dress for beauty's sake alone – colour, texture, and pattern as pure aesthetic expression. In more recent decades, scholars have expanded the list, identifying additional functions such as ornamentation, concealment, social identification, and personal expression. These are the subconscious drivers behind every wardrobe choice – from the statement necklaces to dark hoodies – each serving a deep, psychological purpose; each bewilderingly powerful.

Wellbeing: Hedonic vs. eudaemonic

In fashion psychology, and in this book, wellbeing takes centre stage, but it does so in two distinct acts: hedonic and eudaemonic. *Hedonic wellbeing* is all about pleasure, instant gratification. It's the thrill of the new, the dopamine hit of retail therapy, and the buoyant feeling of biting into a slice of decadent chocolate cake, or that first glass of white wine on a warm summer's day. It's slipping into a fresh new look and realising, with a smug little grin, that it's flawlessly on brand with exactly who you are in this given moment. *Eudaemonic wellbeing*, however, runs deeper. Adopted from Aristotelian thought, it speaks to a more profound sense of fulfilment – personal growth, authenticity, and the pursuit of meaning. In fashion terms, it's the deeply sentimental attachment to your grandmother's scarf or the power you feel in the blazer you wore when you landed your dream job. It's clothing as a vessel for memory, identity, and self-actualisation. Both dimensions reveal how fashion doesn't just make us look good but makes us *feel* good – in ways both fleeting and formative.

And with that, the prelude ends. Now, step forward, reader, as your pursuit begins.

3
Self-expression

Please take your seats

Needless to say, all of us here are, in one way or another, bonded by the unspoken agreement that fashion is far more than just fabric stitched together for modesty or protection. At the very least, it is its own Esperanto. A universal language or visual shorthand that allows us to communicate with one another – sharing secrets, forming friendships, participating in the intricate dance of self-perception and social identity. Lennon (2017) expands on how people use their fashion choices to tango between self-expression and social unity, discussing how "through clothing, individuals can assert uniqueness or conformity, choosing either to stand out or to blend into their social group, depending on their desire for self-expression or belonging". She later elaborates on how "dress can serve as an extension of the self, offering a means for individuals to express their emotions, values and affiliations", illustrating the communicative power of outfit curation that outshines utility and function. And that, my friends, is what we're dedicating this chapter to: the phenomenon of self-expression through clothing, how it stretches far beyond mere aesthetics, and its undisputed ability to transcend all non-verbal methods of self-disclosure.

From the earliest moments in human history, when the only runways were *running away* from all things life-threatening, clothing choices have long been central to the reflection of our self-image and public personas. Historians trace the origins of calculated fashion choices as far back as the Middle Ages, when fashion was first employed as a marker of social standing. The cut, colour, fit and styling of one's attire reflected wealth, status, and occupation, telling a story that words could never fully capture. Today, while perhaps the face of fashion may have evolved, and although we may have abandoned our fig leaves and farthingales (a super-sexy hooped petticoat used in the sixteenth and seventeenth centuries to give skirts a cone or bell shape), self-expression through fashion, at its core, remains ever so en vogue.

Self-expression and social unity: We've touched on the sisterhood between both pillars and how essential the duality is when discussing the psychological implications of fashion. But allow me to ask Big Sis to take centre stage for a moment. A Harvard study has shown that expressing oneself, regardless of the means or medium, triggers the same reward and pleasure centres of the brain as those activated by other fun-tastic experiences – experiences like indulging in a delicious meal, getting money, or – for the purpose of this book, let me put this nicely – *engaging in physical intimacy*. I am fully aware of the fact that this one particular Harvard study may have single-handedly inspired every hip-hop and R'n'B artist circa 1990 to now, but it is, in fact, all true. The act of disclosing information about yourself to an audience, even through non-verbal cues (i.e. fashion), has been proven to bring us emotional satisfaction. Rap about that.

The show is about to start

Having covered a brutally brief history and introduction to self-expression in the realm of fashion, allow me to walk you through the intricately woven sequence of theories, phenomena, and practices that illustrate just how our garments can help us express ourselves and in turn, tap into that mystical sense of wellbeing. Oh, the drama-*turgy* of it all. Read on to get in on why that was oh-so witty:

Beyond the superficial dance of fabrics and colours, fashion is a mirror reflecting our journey of self-discovery. We begin with the most personal of quests, the *discovery* – or in, some cases, myself included, *rediscovery* – of who we truly are and slowly befriending who we hope to be. This is where our journey begins, using fashion and garments to explore our values, quirks, and dreams, and laying the groundwork for what comes next. *Dramaturgy*, darling. With this new sense of self, we take to the world stage, trying on roles ike costumes in a play, each one an experiment in showing off these freshly pressed discoveries, inviting the world to witness how we see ourselves. With every costume change, monologue, and solo, we wait to see if others respond, searching for signs of connection and validation. *Validation*, after all, is an innate and elemental human desire, and with each spark of recognition, each nod of understanding, our self-image tightens its stitches, creating a stronger foundation of *self-perception*. Now, with the remnants of applause echoing within, a clearer, more rooted identity emerges, and we begin to dress with *intention*. And with that, finally, Guy and Banim's work guides us through the importance of dressing with deliberate purpose; aligning outward appearance with inward self-perception (Guy & Banim, 2000). Each stage enriches the next: from self-discovery to social performance, from validation to self-perception, and ultimately to the empowered choice to dress with intention and acceptance. And there it is: a tapestry of self-expression, woven with threads of identity and intention, revealing a truth that transcends the surface: style is more than appearance, it's an assertion of self, stitched together with purpose and passion.

Step I: *Discovery and rediscovery*

I can imagine you're eager to dive headfirst into self-expression, but first, let's take stock of the parts of ourselves we're actually interested in expressing. There's no denying we all have quirks and characteristics that we keep buried deep in our closets – our soon-to-be very psychologically appeasing closets – and perhaps those shadier traits don't belong in the spotlight. Instead, the goal is to step into each day with a positive, authentic, and mindful approach to what we disclose to the world around us, with a clear and unwavering answer to the time-old question: which parts of our identity do we intend on revealing today? And here we go, this is where the journey of self-expression begins. In *Why We Dress the Way We Do* (1985), Ernest Dichter explores how fashion helps us discover, rediscover, and on rare occasions even reinvent aspects of ourselves (Dichter, 1985). He likens the moment of slipping into a garment to unveiling a hidden self, new and alien in an alternate universe – each glance in the mirror revealing a new dimension of who we are is compared to an intoxicating or even hallucinogenic experience. As we shimmy into a new chemise and meet our reflection, we pause, a quiet revelation dawning: "*Ah, so this is part of me, too.*" It's in that fleeting moment of recognition – that's the thrill of discovery.

Fashion's potential as a tool for self-discovery is truly remarkable. Each time we drape ourselves in something new, we are presented with a fresh perspective of our own identity. Much like savouring a foreign dish, wandering onto an enchanting and unfamiliar street, or stumbling upon a song that unexpectedly stirs your soul, the thrill often lies not just in the outcome, but in the act itself, in the unfolding moment of exploration. Science reveals that new experiences invigorate the mind, sharpening our mental agility, and neuroplasticity, helping us remain as adaptable as we are curious. Dr. Gregory Berns, author of *Satisfaction: The Science of Finding True Fulfilment*, shows how new experiences can help form new neural connections and ignite the brain's reward system, unleashing a rush of dopamine, that much-celebrated "happy hormone". Similarly, positive psychology researcher Sonja Lyubomirsky has found that novelty and variety are the secret ingredients to greater happiness and deeper life satisfaction. And really, if we're truly honest with ourselves, isn't that why we're all here, after all?

Fashion, as a form of discovery, allows us to express new facets of our individuality – our personal signature in a world of trends and twinning. When we choose to put on something different, we reclaim our individuality, countering the pressure to conform. So, dear reader, from here on out, dare to disrupt the routine: trade the jeans for that skirt that's been on the back of your mind (and closet) for the last year or so, or let a pair of red shoes electrify the simplicity of the timeless black dress. Stand before the mirror, confront the shift, and let the thrill of discovery wash over you as you realise that "yes, this too, is me."

Discovery, however, is just the beginning. Once we've caught a glimpse of our shiny new characteristics, we can turn our gaze inward and use those same garments to rediscover who we are – fragments of ourselves that may have been forgotten, overlooked, or suppressed. Dichter reminds us that fashion is so much more than just projecting an image; it is also a deeply personal journey of reconnection and reconciliation. In the end, what I personally consider to be the cornerstone of all this, is that to truly be able to express who we are, we need to get to know us, and quite frankly, I've come to learn that that can be one of the most rewarding and liberating of all human experiences. What a privilege it is to get to know ourselves over and over again – to get reacquainted with all our favourite hobbies, traits, scents, and sensitivities that make us truly special. And what greater tool than fashion to guide us through it all? As Joanne Entwistle so aptly puts it in *The Fashioned Body:* "We occupy multiple positions in the world; we have multiple roles that we play (Entwistle, 2000). Identity is always in process. We're always changing, we're always evolving, but identity is stabilised through clothing."

Step II: *Dramaturgy*

So, you're diving deep into your inner world, revelling in the bright and brilliant new facets of who you are – and that's exciting, isn't it? But here's where all the questions come creeping in, like: Why bother sharing any of it? Why put your fresh and shiny self on display for the world to see? It's awfully tempting to keep that special "new you" tucked away and under wraps, like the new book you stumbled on before it becomes a horribly casted Netflix special, or that obscure new remix of that sensational nostalgic track that you want to keep all to yourself before it becomes a permanent resident of your younger brother's shower-time playlist. But here's the thing – it's all about the Dramaturgy, darling. Just like an actor stepping onto the stage, your outfit choices and your actions are part of a bigger performance. It's not about protecting your true self; it's about deciding how you want to show up for the world at any given moment, and why you want to leave your mark. Dramaturgy is sociology's way of saying, "life's a stage, and we're all in the spotlight". Every day is a never-ending performance, where we're constantly slipping into and out of costumes, each one tailored to the roles we're about to play. This phenomenon, coined by sociologist Erving Goffman, suggests that we all have a little director who's set up shop in our heads, nudging us to tweak our outfits based on what's expected in each scene.

The theatre lights go off. and a single spotlight directs your attention to the left of the stage: fashion psychology waltzes in. This is when we truly establish that clothes are more than just fabric, but rather our daily alchemy, transforming us into the versions of ourselves that we – and our little director – wish to project. Each piece in our wardrobe is now a talisman, a carefully chosen part of our armour and allure. Draped in a blazer, we're conjuring the spirit of composure and conviction, as if whispering: "I am exactly where I'm supposed to be", summoning the traits associated with productivity, perseverance, and passion. Telling the world we deserve a seat at the table and demanding respect in return. Alternatively – because we're all complex. multifaceted creatures – when we slip into something softer, cosier, perhaps even vulnerable, we're preaching: "I am a regal spirit deserving of endless sustenance, softness, and luxuries galore". And in turn, we are rallying a community of fellow murder mystery-loving individuals who appreciate slow Sunday mornings and the subjectivity of chocolate "serving sizes". Dramaturgy reminds us that dressing is both an art and an invocation – a way of stepping into the roles we play with confidence, and a silent invitation for others to see us as we wish to be seen. Fashion, then, is not merely an act of covering or concealing; it's a deliberate casting of ourselves as the heroes in our own unfolding stories.

Step III: *Standing ovations*

Now that we've unpacked the art of discovering and rediscovering ourselves – curating traits like a gallery of masterpieces to dazzle the world or simply to provoke calm and composure – it's time to turn from the self to the social. This is where the plot shifts from *me* to *we*. This idea will resurface in more depth when we explore *Social Unity* and how fashion sharpens our sense of belonging and, essentially, how it cements our connection to the collective. But since we're already neck-deep in identity talk, let's start laying the groundwork here.

The theatre analogy continues. Only this time, you've come to the end of the monologue, solo or ferociously elaborate dance routine: your life's stage is set, the curtain rises, and your audience erupts in applause, a symphony of approval. A standing ovation isn't just about admiration, it's about understanding. It's when the crowd doesn't just see you, they *get* you. Every sparkle, every stitch of your outfit speaks volumes, and the response you get?

That kaleidoscope of energy that transcends any and all distance and space between you? That's the power of resonance. Allow me to share a little story with you, a 'case study', if we want to get technical about it. This is the story of Sophia.

At 27, Sophia was at a turning point. As a junior architect at a boutique design firm, Sophia spent her days transforming blank spaces into beautiful blueprints. But beyond the corners of her tiny desk space, she often felt like a work-in-progress herself. As a self-proclaimed introvert, she was at peace with the fact that social gatherings weren't exactly her forte; she'd often opted for sketching façades than navigating small talk. But when her best friend announced her engagement party – a glamorous rooftop soirée brimming with chic twenty-somethings and well-connected thirty-somethings – Sophia knew she couldn't blend into the background or call in with the infamous *cough cough* "I'm sick" Mean Girls excuse. Nerves at the ready, she decided it was her chance to step into the spotlight, both literally and figuratively.

Her goal for the happy occasion was to channel confidence and all things sophisticated, with just enough approachability to keep her grounded. She envisioned herself as the leading lady in a Rom-Com: A cocktail of Meg Ryan meets Sandra Bullock with a splash of Mediterranean heritage and a touch of botox-aphobia. Casting called for someone magnetic, relatable, and undeniably chic. For her "costume", Sophia slipped into her navy blue jumpsuit with a neckline that toed the line between elegant and bold. The fit accentuated her upper body – highlighting her favourite

physical traits and dedication to the pilates studio next door – and flowed comfortably to the ground, creating the illusion of a gown but offering the whimsy and utility of a pair of pants. And it had pockets. Pause for applause. She completed the ensemble with silver pumps and a matching purse. But the pièce de résistance, the one accessory that tied it all together, was her late grandmother's brooch. An ode to the woman who always made her feel like the light of the world, a princess, a woman. And with that subtle battle cry of courage, Sophia was ready.

Before stepping out, she lingered in front of the mirror one last time, adjusting her hair and eyeing her reflection. She imagined how the evening would play out and asked herself if this was the story she wanted to tell tonight, if this was the part of herself she was willing to share. Her reflection gleamed back at her, and with a small, nervous smile, she nodded.

Arriving at the venue, Sophia felt the familiar nerves trickling through her body; nothing like the much-desired butterflies we all long for in a romantic relationship, these were dragonflies making their way aggressively through, around and about her midsection. Sounds fun, doesn't it? Worry not, though, because as soon as she walked into the crowd, the air shifted. Heads turned, eyes lit up, arms waved in chaotic unison, and a soft ripple of admiration moved through the room. One person after another gravitated towards her, drawn not just to her outfit but to the light and confidence it radiated through her welcoming and approachable body language. Conversations flowed almost endlessly, each more effortless than the last. And compliments, so many "incredible-s" and "beautiful-s" and "wow-s". The room buzzed with laughter and energy, and Sophia found herself at the heart of it all. Much to her surprise, a new but familiar comfort – like a part of her that had awakened after a long, deep slumber.

As the evening came to an end, Sophia stepped away from the lively conversations and the laughter that bubbled around her like champagne, and found herself leaning against the terrace railing and taking in the cool breeze and city skyline. In that moment, Sophia felt an unmistakable warmth. Validation. The applause hadn't been literal, but it was there; a cascade of connection, a standing ovation in smiles and sincerity. For the first time in what seemed like an eternity, Sophia didn't just wear the outfit; she lived it.

Sophia's experience – a symphony of giggles and great conversation – is the perfect example of a standing ovation. A truly theatrical *brava!* It's an unspoken agreement between me and my audience that who I am trying to be through my dress and outfit choices is not just well-received, but also deeply understood. And it's here that sociologist Gregory P. Stone's 1962 concept of *programme* and *review* steps into the limelight. Stone, the ultimate style dramaturge, explained that every sartorial choice is a conversation between self and society. This conversation unfolds in two acts:

1. **Programme:** This is your internal assessment; the moment you look in the mirror and ask if the outfit you've chosen reflects who you want to be today.

2.   **Review:** This is the external feedback; how others react to your outfit and, by extension, the version of yourself you have chosen to present to the world in that given moment.

For your social identity to feel validated, the *programme* and *review* need to align. Your intentions need to harmonise with the impressions you leave behind. It's more than just being seen; it's about being seen *correctly*. Psychologist Joanne Eicher expanded on this brilliant phenomenon in 1992, emphasising how our expectations of others' reactions influence what we wear (Eicher, 1992). She explains:

> "Stone labelled the communication of the self through dress as an individual's *programme*. The appraisal of an individual's *programme* is called a *review*. On the basis of their experience through time with other people, individuals develop, in advance of interaction, notions of how other people are likely to react to their dress. If a person's predictions of reactions by others are accurate, the identity or identities this person intends to present via dress aligns with what others perceive. This alignment is what Stone refers to as the validation of the self."

Lo and behold, we're back to where we started. I truly hope you're soothing your goosebumps at how this all came back, full circle. Once we experience that sense of validation, we are fuelled with the confidence to discover, rediscover, and cement who we are, and once more, take the stage. In short, fashion, in the arena of self-expression, is less about draping the body and more about crafting a narrative. The S'Sisters – Self-Expression and Social Unity – are co-writers of the same script. When their lines sync, when the *programme* and *review* are in perfect harmony, it's not just fashion, it's theatre. And you, dear reader, are the star.

Step IV: *Self-perception*

So, what happens after the applause fades and the curtains close? Once the spotlight dims, you're left with the quiet, steady hum of your thoughts. We're all familiar with those ultra-dramatic moments in the movies when the star of the show takes a painfully raw moment to face their reflection in the trailer, questioning everything. Questioning their excellence and mere existence. Self-perception is that backstage mirror, the lens through which we see ourselves after the programme has been performed and reviewed. Right here and now, the world is silenced. While that applause and validation from others might embolden us, it's our own perception of who we are that cements our identity. Those fleeting moments spent tête-à-tête with yourself in the trailer, or dressing room, or bedroom, or car are when we can truly pause for a moment, take a deep breath and say: *well hello there, gorgeous.*

Now answer me this, tucking our little theatre, movie, and drama analogies away – cue the Oscar-worthy scarf toss – if your wardrobe could talk, what would it say? Would it whisper stories of quiet confidence? Would it scream rebellion and red madness from the rooftops? Or maybe, would it mutter anxieties tucked away behind oversized sweaters and darker tones? Contrary to popular belief the clothes we wear don't just *reveal* who we are, they actively *shape* who we believe ourselves to be.

This brings us to the fascinating interplay between fashion and self-perception. Where dramaturgy is about the story you tell the world, self-perception is about the story you tell yourself – and more importantly, the one you wholeheartedly believe. As psychologist Daryl Bem's *Self-Perception Theory* (1972) reveals, humans are more than just spectators of their behaviour; they're analysts. Much like we infer traits about others based on their actions, we do the same for ourselves. *Self-Perception Theory* suggests that when internal cues – emotions or motivations, for example – are weak or ambiguous, we rely on external behaviours to make sense of who we are. Some of you might be reading this thinking that instances like these are minimal, if not completely insubstantial, and if so, good for you. Really, wow. But if any of you are like me and suffer from occasional, if not constant, moments when my innermost motivations, thoughts, and feelings translate to gibberish and moonwalking out of crowded rooms, then do yourselves a favour and keep reading. Sometimes we struggle to *feel* confident and then *act* confident; sometimes, the action needs to come first, and then that steady, unshakable confidence comes through. Think of it like reverse engineering your personality. The idea is to use your wardrobe as more than just a passive collection of garments, and more of an active participant in shaping your identity. Once we welcome the notion that the process of getting dressed, shopping, or even reorganising our closets has a profound impact on helping us be who we truly want to be, it no longer becomes a matter of styling looks, or feeling cute; it's a strategy.

Take, for example, a moment when you need to show up; show up for the day, for those around you, for yourself. Your energy levels are low, and if you could have it your way, the only rules you'd follow for the day are those on the baked potato recipe you've got bookmarked somewhere: the one that demands you let the potato rest for a little while. But instead, you summon all the strength you can muster, and you *reverse engineer:* What does showing up look like? Who do I want to be? Who do I *believe* I can be today? You slip into a vintage band t-shirt, the one with the slightly faded logo of that artist who shaped your teenage years. You style it on your favourite pair high-waisted jeans – because today, we know better than to give in to the low-rise madness – and you tie the whole look together with that fabulous shoulder bag you sourced from that vegan leather store on your last *real* vacation. It's more than just an outfit, it's a wearable time capsule; a quiet manifesto of who you are and what you value. In the mirror, staring back at you, you see someone who cares about sustainability, about authenticity, about honouring their story, and about showing up. In this moment, your brain – forever the enthusiastic curator – decides that this is who you truly are. That this is an honest depiction of your roots, your values, and your journey. And of course, that you look absolutely adorable. And just like that, a simple and almost secondary set of choices in clothing fills you with light and energy. This becomes the way you *act* like you can move forward, even if you didn't feel it to start.

Sounds a little too good to be true, doesn't it? The science behind this shows that when you wear something that resonates with your ideal self, your brain rewards you with a feel-good cocktail of dopamine and serotonin. You are charged with feelings of confidence, a sense of alignment settles in, and suddenly, you're moving through the world with purpose and ease. That shift empowers us to face challenges head-on, seize the day, and step into roles we once doubted we could fill. When we dress in alignment with who we are – or who we dream of becoming – we're not just reflecting our aspirations, we're actively stepping into them, one shoe at a time. What's absolutely terrifying, however, is the extent to which the reverse effect is true too. When you wear something that clashes with how you see yourself, it's as if your entire psyche screams in dissonance. That tension moves well beyond the surface level; it seeps into your emotional and psychological state and can prompt a multitude of horrible physiological reactions. As Johnson and her colleagues (2014) explain, our clothes are a symbolic extension of our identity. When that extension is misaligned, we risk triggering anxiety, a sense of disconnect, or even physical responses like stress eating, irritability, or dips in self-esteem. At the risk of this getting any darker or scarier than it already is, just take note of one last thing: dressing for how you see yourself, who you believe yourself to be, isn't just sartorial, it's psychological. And it's incredibly powerful. Because should that harmony fall out of sync, it's not just your outfit that feels wrong, it's your entire being.

So, what does science have to say about this phenomenon that straddles the fabric of our wardrobes and the depths of our psyche? Fashion psychology researchers like Johnson, Lennon, and Rudd (2014) have explored how clothing serves as more than a social signal, but rather as a mechanism for self-definition in their work on the social psychology of dress. Johnson and her colleagues (2014) dedicated their work to understanding the extent to which the outfits we choose don't just reflect who we are, but also the extent to which they can shape who we believe ourselves to be. Research of this nature has shown us time and time again that what hangs and sits in our wardrobes are artefacts of our identity: the crisp white shirt that provokes your inner Parisian intellect, or the tea dress that helps you feel like you've tumbled out of a romantic novella, delicate yet daring. Before we move on, take a moment, put pen to paper and answer this: Which items of clothing do you own that make you feel *most* like yourself? You know you feel it, you know you recognise that wave of confidence and power rush through you when you put it on. Identify which pieces in your wardrobe speak to that, and what they say about the person you're becoming.

Some of you might be panicking, concerned with the fact that you've never experienced that euphoric sensation before, or that maybe, you're just feeling an immense amount of guilt for spending last month's paycheque on a shopping haul of the exact same items you've been buying since 2009. There, there, no need to panic. For starters, you're here, willing to learn and grow and expand your fashion and psychological horizons. So, there's no going back now, only ever-forward. Research conducted by Davis and Lennon (1985) builds on Bem's *Self-Perception Theory* (1972) and discusses that yes, individuals often gravitate towards clothing that aligns with their *self-concept*, but it's never static. Our wardrobe, much like our inner dialogue, evolves, grows, and occasionally contradicts itself. So fear not, dear reader, you might not have felt *it* yet, but you still can. And you definitely will. Case in point? Read on, and dare you to keep it together:

Isabel was a woman with answers, a therapist in the making in her early thirties who had the ability to untangle anyone's emotional knots but struggled to navigate her own. Vulnerability, especially the romantic kind, wasn't just her Achilles' heel; it was her kryptonite. She couldn't

see herself as a "romantic", let alone someone deserving of that happily ever after – her words, not mine. So, when the man infamously nicknamed 'Mr Green-Flags' insisted on yet another first-date, Isabel found herself at a crossroads between her two selves: the stoic, structured professional she knew so well, the version of herself that she'd dedicated decades on building and bolstering, and then there was 'Little Bella'; the open-hearted dreamer she wasn't sure she could trust.

She turned to her wardrobe for answers and found question marks hung comfortably on the closet rods. A glorious selection of blazers, pencil skirts, shirts and tailored pants that looked like something out of a walk-in catalogue. None of them, however, spoke to the version of Isabel that she secretly hoped to meet that evening – a woman who could be warm, approachable, flirty and feminine, and just a little daring. But then, tucked away behind the sea of navys and greys was a little dress from way back when. You know the one; the one that you get on that trip to the mall with your sister, girlfriend, or overly-friendly sales assistant. The one with the tag still on it. *That* dress. It wasn't a gown or some Cinderella moment, but it was magic all the same: soft fabric that moved just enough to hint at playfulness and vulnerability but held a structure that kept Isabel feeling grounded and safe. Romantic, but not cliché. *That* dress. It was a subtle reminder that sometimes, when you don't feel like the person you want to be, or you're thinking that maybe you don't deserve those things, that it all might be too good to be true, the least you can do is look the part.

And as Isabel slipped into the dress, something shifted. For the first time, she didn't just see someone who could be loved – she felt like someone who deserved it.

A year later, Isabel is happy in her relationship with 'Mr Green-Flags'. They are comfortable, content, and curious about the world together – again, her words not mine. One evening, as she gets ready for date night, she puts on that same dress and lets that newly familiar wave of femininity, romance, and girlish whimsy wash over her once more. Only this time, this dress will come to represent so much more than she could have ever anticipated. On that night, 'Mr Green-Flags' got down on one knee and asked Isabel to be his wife. As she nodded in sheer disbelief and as the words 'yes yes yes' made their way out between bursts of sobs and laughter, she felt her dress soar and dance and fly between hugs and jumps and twists and twirls. In that moment, it became more than an outfit; it was a totem, a reminder of the night she leaned into the kind of vulnerability that builds bridges instead of boundaries. For Isabel, that dress wasn't just a dress – it was possibility, stitched together with courage and hope. The best part? The dress was white.

These stories remind us of a profound truth: the journey to becoming who we always dream of being often begins with recognising a version of that self reflected in the bedroom mirror. It starts with adding flesh and fabric to fantasy. And fashion, when wielded with intention, isn't just an aesthetic choice, it's a deliberate act of self-creation. Consider it a cognitive shortcut to becoming who you've always aspired to be. Fashion allows us to step into the shoes – sometimes, quite literally – of who we hope to be and, in doing so, helps that vision take root. Yes, this is self-perception. But it's also self-actualisation in fabric form; a way of dressing not just for the day but for the life you're building.

Step V: *Dressing with intention*

As we bring this chapter to a close, allow me to circle back to the start one last time, if anything, for the sole purpose of illustrating how far we've come. From that first moment when you feel connected to an item of clothing, when that sensation transcends from skin to soul, fashion becomes a personal compass, guiding you through the galaxy of self-discovery. It becomes a celebration of your quirks, your deepest passions, and your values – whether by rekindling your old connections or boldly exploring new dimensions, daring to venture into uncharted territories of who you are and who you could be. And like a garden in bloom, your wardrobe grows and changes with you; ever-evolving, transforming the abstract and unseen into something strikingly tangible. As the ongoing story of who you are continues, chapter after chapter, we continue to explore our potential, reclaim forgotten aspects of ourselves, and reveal our many selves to the world. Whether consciously curating a look or unconsciously exposing our thoughts and emotions, we express. We share. We indulge in the external manifestation of our internal dialogue. And when done right, we thrive.

The age-old question still lingers: What comes next? After embracing the endless cycle of discovery, rediscovery, seeking validation, faking it 'til we make it, and finally accepting who we are and who we can become – what now? What's waiting for us on the other side of this journey? Here's the truth, dear reader: this is where the magic begins. Welcome to the realm of *dressing with intention*.

This isn't a whimsical idea; it's a concept rooted in psychological research. In their groundbreaking 2000 study, Alison Guy and Maura Banim explored this phenomenon in depth, uncovering some of the most profound insights to date. Their research delves into the dynamic relationship between clothing and the self, revealing how we can consciously harness fashion to present, transform, and even *curate* our identities with purpose and power. Guy and Banim conducted a thorough investigation over several weeks, combining a mix of personal storytelling, meticulous diaries, and wardrobe deep-dives:

The Personal Accounts: Participants were asked to answer the question, *"What do clothes mean to me?"*

The Clothing Diaries: Daily logs chronicling outfit choices and the reasoning behind them.

The Wardrobe Interviews: Explorations of participants' current clothing collections and what they said about their identities.

And from this treasure trove of data, the researchers unearthed a dynamic, multifaceted relationship between clothing and self-perception, distilling their findings into three distinct categories:

The woman I hope or want to be

In this category, women revealed that they used clothing as a tool for crafting positive self-projections. Carefully curated outfits made up of those pieces that make us feel like the stars of our own music videos; the garments that are never truly complete without a cheeky wink in the mirror and a strut and sashay out the door. Most women identified their *favourite* items of clothing as bridges between the person they are and the person they aspire to be. For many, this bridge between the present self and the future self starts with a luxury handbag whispering promises of financial success, or a vintage jacket hinting at a more sustainable, considerate lifestyle. But in some cases, they can be so much more. An example that's quite near and dear to my heart focuses on women who choose to showcase their roots by sporting garments from local designers, celebrating their heritage with pride. In the Middle Eastern region, in particular, there is a growing trend of embracing the richness of ancestral stories through fashion, rewriting narratives of shame into tales of triumph. These choices are intentional, meaningful, and deeply connected to the future selves these brilliant women want to embody.

The best part of all this, dear reader, is that you're already ahead of the curve, you're already one step ahead – and looking divine, I might add. Additional research shows that we are more likely to lean into this category when we've made the conscious decision to invest in our psychological and emotional wellbeing. Picking this book up, in and of itself, is evidence that you, yes you, are already one step closer to being your highest, happiest, and most accomplished self.

The woman I fear I could be

Now, to the shadows. To the darker side of our closets, the fears and anxieties that creep in when our wardrobe stages a mutiny. One moment, you're experimenting with a trendy piece bought impulsively online, or throwing on a shirt from some hazy, way-back-when days. But something's off. Something doesn't quite fit right, it doesn't quite *feel* right. And as the hours tick by, your mood begins to shift. You find yourself slowly morphing into that cranky, irritable, icky version of yourself that you'd much rather leave in the archives. And suddenly, she's front and centre; aggressively honking at cars in traffic, hiding those cookie wrappers in the bin, and screening your sister's phone calls. But fear not, it's not just you, and we're here to help, remember? The first step is recognising the problem. Guy and Banim captured this phenomenon perfectly: the moments when clothing fails to deliver the desired look, or worse, drags you into a spiral of negative self-presentation. This category is dedicated to when our outfits become unintentional mirrors of our insecurities – reflections we didn't sign up to see.

These instances manifest themselves in so many different ways. Sometimes, it's as simple as a garment that doesn't fit as well as we'd hoped. But more often – and more painfully – it's clothing that carries the weight of old wounds. Take, for example, Jasmine. A young woman who once cocooned herself in oversized black clothing during her struggle with depression and disordered eating. Today, after years of therapy, intentional healing, and self-care, she refuses to own anything black, let alone oversized. Even as a happy, healthy woman, slipping into those styles feels like cracking open a door she worked so hard to keep shut. It's akin to catching the scent of an ex's cologne or hearing *that* song after a bad break-up. The brain, ever dramatic, cannot distinguish between memory and reality, and in an instant, the body floods with cortisol, sadness, and unease. And there you are, inhabiting the very version of yourself you thought you'd left behind – proof that clothing can carry echoes of who we once were, for better or worse.

The woman I am most of the time

And just like Goldilocks, we end our little endeavour with the perfect compromise: the woman you are *most of the time*. This is not about aspiration or fear, it's about authenticity. Guy and Banim describe this as a dynamic relationship with clothing, where the greatest joy comes from using outfits to explore and celebrate the multifaceted self. A collection of eccentric, whimsical, safe, and nostalgic bits and pieces that feel like the icing atop a feisty, and ever-so-mighty cake. For Farrah, this meant balancing her dual identities. By day, she's a finance professional navigating a world of grey suits and corporate expectations. But beneath the surface lies a vibrant lover of travel, culture, and the arts. The goal was to create a wardrobe that married these two sides of her personality – to make the woman she is most of the time authentic and appealing to both her personas. The banker and the backpacker. Her professional attire now features playful twists: a pop of colour in her shoes, asymmetric dresses, and eccentric brooches that nod to her love of creativity. Most of the time, you can count on spotting Farrah grabbing her fourth coffee of the day in between meetings in a grey set and burgundy shoes. Most of the time, you can talk numbers with her and her chameleon brooch. *Most of the time.*

This is the transformative power of dressing for the person you are most of the time. It's about building a wardrobe that anchors you in stability while leaving space for those small, joyful moments that make life feel complete. It's where self-expression meets emotional resonance, resulting in a style that feels as authentic as it is empowering. The mission, now, becomes clear: dress for who you are today, who you hope to become, and avoid the reflection of who you fear you could be. This trifecta of intentional dressing doesn't just shape how others see us, it fortifies how we see ourselves. The idea of "Manifestation Dressing", which we'll delve into further in the 'Targeting Goals' chapter, is rooted in this very philosophy – aligning your wardrobe with your aspirations and embodying your dreams through your clothes. But for now, let's pause on the present: the person you are most of the time. She deserves the spotlight. She deserves a wardrobe that celebrates her strengths and sustains her through life's ebbs and flows. And no one brings this philosophy to life more vividly than Maya.

Maya's story is a masterclass in Guy and Banim's framework of self – the woman she fears she's becoming, the woman she hopes to be, and the woman she is most of the time. Each chapter of her wardrobe journey reveals a layer of her identity, showing us how clothing can either shatter or shape the sense of self. Sit back, grab that soothing cuppa-tea, and read on to see how Maya navigated the three categories and reclaimed her style – and herself – along the way. Happy reading.

When Maya first became a mother, she threw herself into the role with unwavering dedication. Now, if you knew Maya, you'd know that this comes as no surprise: Maya, without exception, has taken every chapter and challenge in her life head-on. Hardworking, accomplished, inspiring and aggressive, in every sense of the word. A powerhouse of a woman. She is and always has been the definition of a go-getter and always looked fabulous doing it. So, when

Maya first discovered she was pregnant, it was just another gloriously oversized hat she was proud to put on. But we all know, or should know, that pregnancy is hard. Having a baby is hard. Being a mother is h-a-r-d. And as Maya dove headfirst into the mom-jeans, she unintentionally lost something else along the way – her sense of self. Her wardrobe became a reflection of her exhaustion: shirts decorated in spit-up, leggings that could make anyone question the concept of elasticity, and – I kid you not, she squirmed when she said this – Crocs. Each garment told the story of a woman deep and drowning in "mommy mode". The "mommy mode" she swore she'd never succumb to. The "mommy mode" her own mother blamed her for.

Looking in the mirror, she struggled to see Maya. *Maya* Maya, not Mommy Maya. She felt lost. Disheartened. She felt surrounded by a visual echo of her school days, when late nights, fatigue, and bullying left her with painfully low self-esteem. The feelings were all too familiar, and the sight of her dishevelled self brought them rushing back. You see, Maya grew up as the quintessential "good girl". Her parents believed in discipline and practicality, favouring plain clothing that left no room for self-expression. Her wardrobe was as muted as her voice in a household where individuality took a backseat to "yes ma'am" and academic perfection. At school, her lack of armour made her an easy target, and she endured relentless torment that chipped away at her already fragile self-esteem.

But when she left for college – fleeing her country, her hometown, and the torment of her schoolmates – Maya finally found freedom. She painstakingly rebuilt her confidence, brick by brick, day to night, adorning herself in clothes that declared her worth before she ever spoke a word. She became the woman she always wanted to be – self-assured, vibrant, unshakable, brilliant. But now, the self-assured college student was buried under piles of laundry, unrecognisable with a wardrobe she no longer resonated with. Maya's clothing had become a reflection of her insecurities, a portal back to her past, whispering doubts and fears she thought she'd left behind.

Her experience was far from exceptional, and it most certainly wasn't her fault. Don't just take my word for it – I've brought the science to back it up. In 2013, Jennifer Ogle and her team expanded on Guy and Banim's concept of the self to investigate how clothing consumption impacts identity during life's major transitions, like pregnancy (Ogle, Tyner, & Schofield-Tomschin, 2013). Sarcastic *"surprise, surprise"*, it's no smooth sailing. The study uncovered a common struggle; women often find themselves battling against the limited maternity options available. These options failed to align with their evolving identities, offering few choices that aided in their transition. Not who they were before, not who they were becoming, and certainly not the woman they hoped to be post-baby. Instead of being a tool and source of comfort, these garments amplified insecurities, leaving women stuck in a liminal phase that felt isolating and disorienting.

And then the baby arrives. Between sleepless nights, endless feedings, and the sheer mental and emotional load of new motherhood, who has the energy to overhaul a wardrobe? So, inevitably, you grab that spit-up-stained tee, you stress, sigh, and keep moving. And the cycle continues, day in and day out. At least it did for Maya.

But Maya wanted to be a mother. And Maya wasn't ready to settle for this version of herself, drowning in exhaustion and self-neglect. Maya wanted it all. She envisioned a mother her kids could look up to, someone who embodied the idea that you *can* have it all – a thriving career, a loving marriage, a healthy lifestyle, and a strong sense of self. She craved balance in every aspect of her life: family, friends, fashion, finances. All of it. She wanted it so badly. For herself, yes, but more so, for her daughter. Maya wanted to show her that breaking cycles was possible – the cycle of losing oneself in trying times, and the echoes of her own childhood, where self-expression was stifled. And Maya swears she felt it happen – a shift so profound it was almost physical – the moment she slipped into her linen set. That was the day she reclaimed herself and redefined what motherhood would look like to her. The gap between who she was and who she wanted to be, was slowly but ever so surely, closing up.

Clothing became her tool for transformation. She was drawn to linen sets and wrap dresses – pieces that exuded effortless elegance, simplicity, and saved up those precious moments of silence by taking the guesswork out of getting dressed. Matching sets became her secret weapon. She floated in neutral hues. Her newfound aesthetic was *La Maman Chic* in linen, silk, and cashmere. She had found her middle ground: the woman she is most of the time is truly

peaceful and powerful. For Maya, dressing with intention has become a daily affirmation, and her wardrobe a testament to her journey. As she unpacks her closet, preparing for her first big move since getting married, Maya folds away her old school sweater, a concert tee from her college days, her suits, dresses, heels, and blazers. Maya packs her linen sets and wrap dresses. She's on the bedroom floor in a cashmere ensemble, and seated next to her, fidgeting with a canvas tote, is her baby girl, dressed in an identical vanilla set.

I hope, since you're reading this, you now know so much more about self-expression than ever before. That time-old "fashion makes me express myself" response, drenched in ambiguity and misunderstanding, will make you roll your eyes pretentiously, but also giggle in knowing that you, yes you, now know what that *really* means. Tell them. Tell them it's never just fabric; it's the threads of who we are, the layers of who we've been, and the outlines of who we aspire to become. Tell them to dress is to declare. Tell them that it's more than just an act of covering the body; it's a performance, a ritual, a reckoning with the self. That each garment we choose becomes a participant in the grand theatre of our lives, shaping and reshaping the story we tell.

This chapter has been about more than just self-expression; it's been about self-perception, validation, and transformation. We've explored the delicate dance between the selves we inhabit and the selves we long for, the moments when clothing becomes our ally or betrays us, and the extraordinary power of dressing with intention. We've cemented the initial notion that fashion is not frivolous; it's foundational. It has the ability to unearth buried insecurities, bolster fragile confidences, and bridge the gap between the person we are today and the one we hope to be tomorrow. And with that, the invitation is this: step into your wardrobe with courage. Let your clothing validate who you are, celebrate who you've been, and illuminate the path to who you're becoming. Dress for power, for peace, for joy. Dress for the moments you'll never forget and the ones you're still daring to dream of. Let every stitch, every seam, every texture be a declaration that you are here, you are whole, and that you are, quite frankly, unstoppable.

4
Understanding the body

Our bodies are like handwritten letters – unique, expressive, and deeply personal, and yet we often treat them like unsent love notes, neglected and buried under layers of shame and unrealistic expectations. Body image – a concept defined by our perceptions, thoughts, and feelings about our bodies (Lennon et al., 2017) – is at the heart of this disconnect. This chapter is an invitation to dust off the narrative and rewrite your relationship with your body. Fashion, after all, as a psychological tool, offers so much more than surface-level solutions. It becomes a dialogue, a way to listen to your body, to nurture it, and to celebrate its nuances. By understanding how clothing choices can act as bridges rather than barriers, as confetti, not camouflage, we can cultivate a healthier and happier connection to ourselves.

So, dear reader, make sure you're comfortable, hydrated and ready to gasp in utter shock and disbelief. Before we can work towards solving the problem, allow me to share with you just how truly significant and spine-chilling the problem is. The reality is that body image issues are nearly universal with 35% of adults and over 30% of teenagers reporting feelings of depression or shame about their bodies (Mental Health Foundation,

2019). The consequences of these struggles ripple through our mental health, contributing to concitions like anxiety, depression, and disordered eating. Think about that for a minute: Those statistics translate to a truly heartbreaking reality; if you're out with a group of ten friends, giggling over drinks, or reminiscing at a big family lunch, at *least* three or four of your loved ones are struggling with body image to the point that it's impacting their mental health. And that's just the maths. That means that while the table is full of conversation and clinking glasses, someone is picking at their food, feeling ashamed. Someone else is pulling at their sleeves, adjusting their posture, anxious about being seen. Another might have considered skipping the gathering altogether. This isn't just a personal battle; it's a collective reality – one that keeps people from fully experiencing joy, connection, and even something as simple as a meal with loved ones.

Now, I, personally, have a deep respect for the term and definition coined by Sonya Renee Taylor: body terrorism. Yes, it's dark and dramatic. And yes, it is absolutely necessary. Because, quite frankly, there is nothing 'chic' about heroin. There is no muffin baking atop anyone's jeans. There's no mom bod or dad bod. There's just bod. And that bod is beautiful. Beautiful and brilliant and blameless. So yes, to all the haters and shamers, 'Terrorism' seems more than appropriate. Taylor defines it as the structural marginalisation of bodies based on markers such as race, gender, age and ability. Understanding the forces at play allows us to see that body image isn't just about individual self-perception – it's deeply entangled with societal narratives. So here we are, silencing said narrative and revolting with a newer, kinder, and more compassionate tale. And look, we're serving muffins by the door.

So, how can understanding the body through fashion enhance our wellbeing? How can a selection of shirts and skirts rewrite a story we've been told for decades? Well, it starts by reclaiming clothing as a tool of self-expression rather than self-erasure. Instead of shrinking, masking, or apologising for our bodies, we can dress to celebrate them. From ditching the tyranny of vanity in favour of a 'fit-first' approach to understanding the fine line between body neutrality and body positivity, fashion becomes the ultimate vehicle for self-acceptance. And if strutting in form-fitting clothing feels like too big a leap, even the smallest acts like experimenting with makeup, accessories, and hairstyles can be the stepping stones towards the marvellous and magical moments of self-celebration.

This chapter, therefore, isn't just about body image – it's about liberation. We'll unpack what body image truly is, how it shapes our mental wellbeing, and the ways fashion can become a tool of empowerment rather than restriction. You will learn how something as simple as opting for the right fit, embracing body neutrality, or shifting your internal dialogue can change not just how you dress. but how you feel in your own skin. With the help of real-life case studies, we will prove that fashion isn't trivial – it's transformative. Because at the end of the day, understanding your body isn't about fitting the mould – it's about breaking it.

The mirror, the myth, the mindset: *What is body image?*

Consider, if you will, the moment you catch your reflection in a passing window. In the grand scheme of things. it's a passing glance, and yet it has the power to dictate your mood, posture, perhaps even your entire day. Ah, body image. A term tossed around so casually in conversations about self-esteem, yet rarely dissected with the precision and understanding it deserves. At its core, body image is not merely about how we look; it's about how we *perceive* ourselves, how we *feel* about those perceptions, and how those feelings shape the way we move through the world. It is a symphony of psychology, experience, and cultural influence, conducted by none other than…you. Yes, just little old you. Shocking. Isn't it? Considering that, admittedly, society is often rudely trying to grab the baton.

If we were to get technical about it – and this is a legitimately educational book after all – esteemed psychologist P.D. Slade (1994) defines body image as the mental representation one holds of their physique – an intricate construct shaped by a world of influences, including:

Body satisfaction or dissatisfaction: *Often led by the erratic whims of societal ideals and eventually leads to that ever-present gauge dictating whether you feel like a masterpiece or a never-ending work-in-progress.*

Sensory experiences: *How it feels to exist in your body – how the fabric drapes over your skin. Everything from the quiet relief of elastic waistbands, to the autocracy of stiff shirt collars.*

History of weight fluctuations: *Because in the hollow corners of our minds, the ghost of body's past persists.*

Cultural and social norms: *An ever-shifting landscape of beauty standards, none of which ever seem to be particularly invested in our wellbeing.*

Comparisons to others: *The phenomenon of feeling perfectly content until, alas, social media does what it does best.*

Mental wellbeing: *Because the mind and the body are dance partners, but which is in the lead? Now, that's the question.*

Biology and physical health: *Because, as it turns out, our genetics, hormones, and metabolism are immune to the commands of fashion magazines.*

In essence, body image is the ever-evolving mental blueprint of how we see, feel, and think about our bodies. It's not just about liking or disliking what you see in the mirror, it's a complex interplay of perception, emotion, memory, and social influence. It's shaped by past experiences, cultural expectations, biological factors, and even fleeting sensory impressions. It dictates whether we strut into a room with a quiet confidence or take complete ownership of the dark corner by the stairs. And, no surprises here, it not only influences our relationship with fashion, but orchestrates it. For you see, our relationship with our bodies shapes what we wear, yes, but also *how* we wear it; the zip of a jacket, the tilt of a hat, the hesitation or ease with which we slip into a dress. Our clothes become an extension of our self-perception, wrapping us in either self-doubt or self-confidence.

It's this gloriously intricate and intimate kinship between our perception and consequent attitude that psychologists call the 'Attitudinal Component of Body Image'; a fancy and completely intimidating way of referring to how our thoughts can trigger our emotions – emotions that can range from pride and confidence to frustration and shame. In the words of Schurrer (2019), our internal dialogue often acts as both the seed and the sustenance of these perceptions, shaping how we see ourselves and, ultimately, how we feel. Allow me to elaborate and draw from a familiar picture: On the days – I pray they're not many – when those intrusive thoughts worm their way in, hissing things like 'look at that belly', or 'oh God, those thighs' or worst of all, 'I <u>hate</u> myself', do we feel an overwhelming surge of confidence? A rush of joy? Of course not. What follows is a cocktail of shame, embarrassment, frustration, and worst of all, sadness. Thought feeds perception, perception fuels emotion, and emotion dictates experience. It's a domino effect, and when it starts with self-criticism, that fall is far from graceful.

What's more, body image isn't just an internal monologue, it's a full-blown psychological phenomenon with real-world consequences. Research in the *Social Psychology of Dress*, Lennon and her co-authors discuss how our perceptions of the body influence not only how we feel but also how we act. The research shows that our body perceptions drive our levels of satisfaction and dissatisfaction, which in turn influence the choices we make: think of all those times you've felt fabulous and reached for that frilly summer dress or when you gave in to your inner demons and cocooned in an oversized sweater. Individuals content with their physiques may don vivid hues and audacious silhouettes, while those plagued by discontent may retreat to armour of dark, shapeless garments, as if to will themselves into hiding. All our actions, all our choices, all our fits are tethered to this ever-shifting relationship with our reflection.

This raises the inevitable question: When body image falters, what are the ramifications for our mental health, self-perception, and indeed, our very quality of life? How does our body image ripple into who we are and impact the behaviours that pervade our daily lives? And how do we trade the shackles of self-doubt for the bangles of celebration? That's exactly what we're unpacking next.

Body image and wellbeing: *When self-perception meets self-preservation*

If body image is the lens through which we see ourselves, then wellbeing is the light that either illuminates or distorts the view. Our relationship with our reflection holds sway over something far greater than the mirror or our camera rolls, it powers our mental health. It has tangible consequences on our emotional state, cognitive function, and overall quality of life. Negative body image doesn't simply dampen and darken our fashion choices – it discourages and demoralises. It cripples our motivation, our ability to think clearly, and our inherent joie de vivre. But here's *le twist:* the very thing that body image influences – our clothing choices – can, in turn, be wielded as a tool to reclaim control. The right ensemble can be a catalyst for confidence, a conduit for joy and, dare we say, a brain-boosting style secret. I told you this was a happy book.

One of the most delightful nuggets of research I've expanded on myself, to date, stems from Bell, Cardello and Schutz's work on the relationship between perceived clothing comfort and exam performance back in 2005 (Bell et al., 2005). Their study found that the more comfortable students were, the higher their exam scores. Which later inspired my own findings that individuals display heightened levels of cognitive performance when they are comfortable. Now, before we all burn and bury our bras and blazers, there's a bell-curve threshold at play here. When I say *comfortable*, I'm not championing an all-day affair in pyjamas and loungewear – tempting as that may be. True comfort isn't about slouchy sweatpants; it's about the absence of distraction. It's about wearing something that doesn't demand constant tugging, adjusting, or second-guessing. Comfort, in this sense, is a state of ease; a calm, collected, and confident equilibrium that frees up your mental bandwidth for bigger, better things. So before you start swimming in sweats or turn blue suffocating in that size-too-small pair of jeans – *just to cling to the illusion that single-digit dress sizes hold some kind of cosmic power* – remember this: ill-fitting jumpers and those too-tight trousers, just might squeeze out some of your cognitive prowess too, and we don't want that now, do we? Comfort, dear reader, is king.

But it's not just about acing tests and slaying at Sudoku. Therapy programs have demonstrated remarkable effectiveness in enhancing body satisfaction and self-concept. Participants often describe the daily ritual of dressing up as a delightful indulgence – a moment of *me time* that transforms clothing into a life-affirming, body-positive experience. This sartorial self-care, in turn, has been proven to ignite creativity, foster positive feelings towards the physical self, and effectively counter negative emotions (Lee and Yoo, 2020). But you know I come bearing records to research: Everyone, meet Josie.

Josie never considered herself a vain woman. Practical, yes. Sensible, absolutely. A woman who always had gum to spare and the first to wish friends a happy birthday so that everyone else was sure to follow suit. But vain? Never.

That trait was reserved for the glossy-haired women in magazines, for those who twirled in front of mirrors rather than avoid them. Josie was simply far too busy, far too occupied by the humdrum rhythm of work, family, grocery runs, outdoor runs, Netflix re-runs, and oh-so much more. Or at least, that's what she told herself every morning as she layered herself in whatever outfit would get her out the door fastest. A monochrome look, not because it was Scandinavian-Chic, but because it was easy – effortless, even. Clothes, to Josie, represented pure function, a means to an end, an extension of the coffee mug, the laptop, and the car keys.

But deep down, beneath the practical sweaters and basic tees, there was a silent yearning. A wish that her body didn't feel numb. A longing for a time when getting dressed would be an act of joy, not a meticulous strategy session dictated by what needed to be concealed. Instead, Josie ached to celebrate her body; to shift her focus away from the shape and size and curves and dips of her physique and instead dedicate the art of dressing to a newfound and inspiring mindful ritual. She wanted more for her body. She wanted to silence the voices, cruel and relentless, that turned compliments to scepticism, dressing to an Olympic sport, and had the ability to categorise women like her as no more than treats at a 3-star breakfast buffet: muffins, apples, and pears, oh my! Josie wanted more. But it wasn't until she caught herself mindlessly reaching for the same monochrome – or in her words, "monotone" – outfit again that she realised just how desperate she'd been for change.

Determined to reclaim something – she wasn't quite sure what yet – she felt a shift. The routine started to change. Josie's introduction to fashion psychology was like the first stirring of something deeply transformative. No drastic makeover, no frantic attempt to 'fix' anything, but a quiet, intentional journey to the woman she truly wanted to be. She'd spent so long focusing on what she lacked, on the busy-body she'd become, on work, family, runs, running, and not getting run-over, that she'd forgotten to stop and see what she had. Slowly, hesitantly, she named them: Her eyes, kind and expressive. Her hands, steady and strong. Her collarbone, elegant and understated. It was a small shift, but a profound one.

Over the weeks, Josie learned to dress for the body she had, not the one she used to have or wished for. She played with colours, trading the blacks and greys for deep greens and jewel tones that made those gorgeous eyes shine. She discovered the joy of texture – the softness of cashmere and the crispness of linen. She treated clothing as more than just mere function. She used clothing as a gift to herself, a playful pause in the midst of the madness; the routine had evolved to coffee, clothing, car keys, and confidence. And on a random day thereafter, Josie stood before her wardrobe, conscious of the ticking clock and the inbox that seemed to magically replenish itself, and she paused. She took a deep breath and ran her fingers through her hair and over her arms as though to wash the stiffness of panic away. She opened her eyes to the basics and blazers lined up like loyal soldiers in her closet, pushed them aside with grace

and gratitude, and reached for a new pair of high-waisted embellished jeans. She smiled and ran those same hands over the sparkles: sparkles in celebration of the body, the woman, and the journey.

Body image doesn't always announce itself. It doesn't always stand atop cafeteria tables with a bullhorn and brownies, nor does it linger by the blaring and thundering Juicer 3000, side-eyeing you over the rim of a kale-infused power potion like a self-certified wellness guru. Oh no, sometimes it simply lurks on the sidelines, swaying our choices, dulling our joy, and holding us back in ways so insidious, we'd hardly ever know it. That's why Josie's story is so important. On the surface, she had no distinguishable 'issue' with her body – at least, not one that the world openly defines as an issue. And yet, it dictated her every movement, dimmed little moments, and kept her from fully experiencing life in its wild and wondrous intensity. That's the thing about body image: it isn't about the reflection, it's about restriction. It determines what we wear and how we wear it – whether we sashay in a satin skirt or tug at the hem, or whether we honour ourselves in colour or lay low in "monotone". And while, to some, it might seem trivial, the effects ripple far beyond our wardrobes. When body image stumbles, confidence wavers, opportunities shrink, and our basic birthright to enjoy ourselves becomes a bloody battle. But this cycle can be changed, its entire existence recalibrated. Just as Josie was able to shift her frame of mind and beliefs on her body's frame, you too can ignite a healthy and happy relationship with your body. So, if you're finally ready to rewrite the story of your body; narrate the truths its lines, creases, scars and cracks tell the world, if you're ready to be your own canvas, not captor, then turn the page, take my hand, for this is where your new chapter begins.

Same body, new image: *Rewriting the narrative*

Ah, body image. The ever-present, ever-opinionated houseguest that no one ever actually invited over, and yet, here they are – waltzing in unannounced, wriggling into conversations, and dishing out unsolicited critiques and commentary on what we're all wearing and how we're behaving. And lest we forget that infamous *tsk tsk* – served with a hint of disdain and a generous serving of unadulterated disappointment. But it's quite alright, we're learning to keep our little dinner parties *hush-hush*. We've learnt to dissect its origins, unravel its influences, and lay bare the ways it manifests in our closets, our reflections, and our choices. But now, dear reader, it's time for the pièce de rèsistance – the main event, the guest of honour, the chocolate soufflé – it's time for us to wrest back control. Because, contrary to popular belief, we don't actually have to be at war with our bodies. There are ways – clever, psychological, scientifically backed ways – to shift our perspectives, to trade self-doubt for self-acceptance, to silence that inner critic, to cordially and respectfully throw out the houseguest. And so, without further ado, let's show them the door.

Changing our body image: *From self-doubt to self-devotion*

Embarking on the journey to positive body image requires a lot more than a perfectly curated Pinterest board filled to the brim with inspirational quotes and adorable illustrations. Instead, it demands an understanding of the sneaky societal influences that warp our perceptions alongside a strong and honest commitment to practices that foster self-acceptance. But before you start aimlessly chanting 'I am beautiful, I am strong' to your barely-there reflection in the steam-clouded bathroom mirror, know this, dear reader none of this matters unless you believe you are worthy. Worthy of this journey. Worthy of the words you will speak. Worthy of the love you will bask in. Worthy of the unapologetic, electric sense of joy and confidence that will slowly build on this path and stay with you, always. From vanity sizing to the way we address our bodies, every small shift in perspective can inch us closer to a healthier sense of self. Let's delve into some of the most common culprits of body image distress, and more importantly, let's tackle how to outsmart them.

Vanity sizing: *The fashion industry's pettiest power play*

Number #1 – pun absolutely intended – vanity sizing. The fashion industry's most passive-aggressive mind game. In an effort to stroke consumer egos, brands manipulate size labels, making garments appear larger so we can pat ourselves on the back for squeezing and sucking into smaller sizes. This devious strategy does nothing but reinforce unrealistic standards and trigger squeals, sighs and existential crises in the dressing room. One day, you're a size eight, the next, you're a size twelve, and I can guarantee you nothing has changed but the whims of a retailer. Allow me to conjure up one of those daunting shopping sprees, won't you? You're in a store, arms overflowing with jeans from three different brands. You slip into the first pair – a size eight – only to find that they're almost religiously reluctant to budge past your thighs. Mild panic. You reach for the next pair – a size ten, from another label – and vo là, gliding and sliding on your body like second skin. Relief. But we all know it wouldn't be a *spree* if we didn't try on that third pair; yet another brand, same exact design, size six, all they had in store, and somehow it…fits? Now, instead of revelling in the ecstasy of a successful afternoon and finding a new pair of jeans, you're spiralling into a size-induced identity crisis. Were you always this size? Has your body changed overnight? Could it be the lighting? Or is it the mirrors? The gum you're chewing?

…Sorcery?

There's no magic, just madness – the madness of an industry hell-bent on convincing you that your worth can be neatly packaged into a number, letter, or some arbitrary section at a department store: pretty please, don't call me *petite*. The real magic is found in the sweet, rebellious thrill of outsmarting the system and embracing the 'fit first' approach. Instead of fixating on the number stitched into a waistband, prioritise how a garment feels on your body and how it makes you *feel*. A good fit should complement, not constrict, and comfort is an absolute non-negotiable. If your jeans fit like a dream, make you truly happy, but the tag makes you flinch, cut it out. Literally. No one needs that kind of negativity.

Let that body talk: *Conversations we need to rethink*

Then there's negative body talk – the ex-best friend that somehow manages to turn every coffee date or fitting-room moment into a roast session. We're all guilty of either partaking in it or gawking in silence as it happens around us. The almost reflexive groan at one's thighs or bum or pimple or dimple, or the defeated sigh at a reflection that doesn't quite match the filtered ideal in our minds. We toss out self-criticism so casually, it barely registers as harmful; just background noise in the grand conversation of our lives. But the research is clear: engaging in 'fat talk' or body shaming isn't just idle chatter, it's a direct line to deeper body dis- satisfaction, a slow erosion of self-esteem, and a reinforcement of the very standards we wish didn't exist. Remember that shopping spree we were just on – *see Vanity Sizing above* – now imagine your best friend or sister or daughter in the dressing room next to yours, trying on her own set of jeans. She examines herself in the mirror, mutters something self-deprecating about herself, tugs at the blouse, and pinches at her skin. To you, she is a goddess. A queen. The perfect woman. Instinctively, you leap in with reas- surance, showering her with praise, reminding her of her beauty, frantically trying to drown out her doubt with love. But when you're on your own, facing your own reflection, that kindness rarely extends inward. This kind of self-critique has become so ingrained that generations of young women around the world find it odd and uncomfortable to compliment themselves unless prompted, allowing the narrative to slowly chip away at their self-esteem, one offhand remark at a time. The solution is simple. Just as you leapt at your goddess girlfriend with love and reassur- ance, apply that same intensity to yourself. The moment those mean and malicious voices creep in, shut them down and drown them out with kindness. And if that self-acceptance is a work in progress, if you're in the process of healing and learning to love yourself anew, then start with your circle. Surround yourself with people who celebrate you, who honour their bodies in all their glorious, ever-changing forms. Enrich yourself with people who steer conversation away from the superficial. Because the truth is: our bodies fade, and change, and endure, and survive – but that smile, that glow fuelled by electric, undeniable joy when you call yourself beautiful…now that's forever.

Body ~~positivity~~ neutrality: *The battle between loving and living*

Naturally, of course, this brings us to the ongoing debate between body positivity and body neutrality. While the former preaches unconditional love for every bump and curve, it can sometimes feel like an impossible standard. Instead, consider body neutrality: the more balanced, less exhausting, wiser, older sibling. It shifts away from the impractical expectation of adoring one's reflection day in and day out, and instead, champions respect and appreciation for what the body *does*. The quiet miracles it performs daily. The way your nervous system fires up at a touch, the way your pupils adjust to light, the countless invisible efforts that keep you moving, feeling, and alive. Your legs, for instance, are more than their circumference – they carry you through life, step by step. Your arms hug, create, and express. Your entire body is a roadmap, a tool that tells your story or helps you share it. Body neutrality and fashion, therefore, aren't about adorning every inch of your physique, though if you can, chapeau to you. Instead, it's about dressing in ways that honour your body for its strength, its persistence, its kindness, and its forgiveness. It's about choosing fabrics that soothe, silhouettes that empower, and colours that energise. In truth, using clothing in body neutrality is our way of thanking our bodies for simply *being* and for letting us be.

Why hide when you can highlight: *Using fashion as a declaration, not an apology*

Well, if that isn't the perfect segue into clothing, I don't know what is. The way we dress is one of the easiest ways to boost or bruise our body image, yet so many of us fall victim to using fashion to cover up instead of show up. Yes, we're all tempted to camp out in oversized everything always to feel safe and invisible from the scrutiny of the world, but when it's solely used to hide – versus as a tribute to the rise of oversized fashion in the early nineties – it often reinforces negative perceptions and hinders a development in self-acceptance. Forget dressing to morph into the background or as a means of silencing a story your body can't help but tell – experiment with styles that make you feel *alive;* decorate it in honour of the life you've lived. Play with colours that lift your spirits, textures that beg to be touched, and silhouettes that accentuate your body as it is, not as some impossible ideal. Contrary to popular belief, fashion isn't a battleground, but a playground. So dress like you've come to play.

And if there's anyone who's mastered the game, it's Willow.

For years, Willow stood before the mirror and saw only fragments – a blur of expectations, disappointments, and echoes of a past that had weighed on her shoulders for far too long. The daughter of a diplomat, she was raised in the

language of formality, where self-expression was secondary to decorum and always considered a luxury, never a right. She learned to exist within boundaries, became a master of suppression, and her body had become both a battlefield and a bystander to a life that demanded perfection when all it truly craved was the warm embrace of belonging. And by the age of eighteen, Willow had already lived many lives: the careful child, the obedient daughter, the diligent student. Each version shaped by external pressures, each one moving further away from the young girl who had once twirled in front of her childhood mirror, dreaming of a world that would celebrate her without conditions. By the age of eighteen, Willow's family decided to uproot their lives and move back to their homeland, forcing Willow to face a new and extraordinary upheaval. At the mere, sweet age of eighteen, Willow finally admitted that she was solely put on this Earth to serve – to serve her family, her career, her responsibilities, but never herself. And with that, her body endured: endured the late-night snacks, the dysmorphia, the silent screams, the stress, the sadness, and the strength.

Years later, Willow's body was a source of sorrow. The taunts from childhood still clung to her skin like an old scar, whispering that she was too much, yet somehow never enough. Dressing became an act of concealment rather than celebration. Shopping trips were a silent humiliation – scanning racks for the largest sizes, settling for whatever fit, never daring to choose what she *could* love, or who she *could* be. Fashion was survival, not joy. Dear reader, please try not to misunderstand. Willow was genuinely and undeniably brilliant. An accomplished woman, a corporate powerhouse who had spent years negotiating deals, managing teams, and leading high-stake projects. But no professional success could quiet the relentless inner dialogue that whispered hateful criticisms about her body. No external achievement, goal, or profession could ever make Willow feel truly *alive*.

Today, Willow is seven years old. Yes, I am well aware that mathematics is not my forte, but it's not that bad. Bear with me.

Seven years ago, came a moment of reckoning. Willow made the executive decision to fight for herself. Together with her husband, she underwent major weight loss surgery, an act not of surrender, but of reclamation. Today, Willow admits, "I am only seven years old", with a smile tugging on her lips, "because that's when I truly began to live." But surgery changed only her body. The mind, the heart, the wounds of years spent hiding – those needed a little something more. And that's what Willow decided to invest in her wellbeing, her inner narrative, in loving and caring for that little seven-year-old girl.

Fashion psychology was not a luxury or an indulgent spree through the aisles of high-end boutiques; it was a lifeline. It was months of talk therapy, raw self-reflection, hesitant steps forward, and inevitable stumbles back. It began subtly – a colour here, a texture there. Clothing became more than a necessity; it became a dialect of self-acceptance, a means of reclaiming space in a world that had long told her to shrink. Gone were the days of drowning in shapeless fabric, of hiding beneath layers meant to erase. Now, she demanded presence with the cinch of a waisted jumpsuit, moved with purpose in sleek loafers, and found solace in the steadying symmetry of monochrome. She discovered an anchor in her hands – the same hands that had signed contracts, wiped away tears, and held herself together on the hardest of days. They had never changed, not after the surgery, not after years of self-doubt. And now, they have become a canvas for her growth. A deep burgundy polish for confidence, a soft blush for tenderness, a bold red when she needed reminding of her own fire. At her fingertips, quite literally, was her weaponry, and she built her armour around it.

Today, at seven years old, Willow walks away from the corporate world she once tethered herself to. She is no longer just a participant in her own life; she is its architect. As the proud co-founder and CEO of an investment firm, she moves with certainty, dedicating each morning to the ritual of dressing – a sacred act of self-care she no longer compromises. Her nail polish changes weekly, a silent manifesto of her moods and ambitions, each a shade of promise to herself. Each a starting point to a new outfit.

Tonight, as I sit and write this, Willow is at a concert, bathed in golden lights, her laughter lost in the symphony of voices singing along. She moves freely and carelessly, adorned in embellished trousers that shimmer with every step, and a fitted jumpsuit sculpting the frame she has learned to love. She is, much like her namesake, reborn.

Like the willow tree, she bends but never breaks, her dresses swaying in the wind, fluid yet unwavering. Her shoes are steady, their heels digging into the earth, grounding her with the strength of deep roots and history. Willow is

no longer just surviving; she is alive, thriving, growing, reaching – stretching for the sun.

And if I'm being honest, I, too, can't wait to be seven years old myself someday.

Willow's journey encapsulates everything we've uncovered so far: the weight of societal expectations, the silent battle with one's inner narratives, the way self-worth can be eroded by something as ridiculous as sizing or the pressures of a shopping mall. Her story is one of reclamation, not just of her body, but of her voice, her presence, and her right to take up space exactly as she is. When we first explored body neutrality and the idea of dressing to honour your body rather than conceal it, this is exactly what we meant. Willow underwent weight-loss surgery for her health, not for a dress size, not to conform to an airbrushed ideal, and certainly not because a magazine or an algorithm whispered that she should. Medically, she needed it. But the real transformation wasn't about numbers on a scale – it was about learning to accept herself, regardless of what she looked like. And at the heart of that acceptance was something seemingly small but deeply symbolic: her nail polish. Her entire dress persona revolved around it. Because sometimes, when an entire outfit feels like a tad too overwhelming, we can start with the fingertips, or a swipe of lipstick, or a pinky ring. The smallest details can often hold the greatest power.

Makeup magic: *A love letter in lipstick*

This same philosophy applies to makeup. Ah, makeup – society's most legal and socially acceptable form of alchemy. But beyond their ability to transform a very sleep-deprived mortal into a radiant deity, makeup and skincare have been scientifically linked to improve mental health and self-perception. Studies – yes, actual science, not just the gospel according to Sephora – suggest that the physical act of applying makeup or indulging in a skincare routine can be downright therapeutic. The *Journal of Aesthetic Nursing* notes that makeup application boosts self-esteem, providing a sense of control over one's appearance. Because, let's be honest, there's something profoundly stabilising about a perfectly executed cat-eye in an otherwise utterly maddening world. Skincare, on the other hand, is basically mindfulness in a bottle: the rhythmic motions of cleansing, moisturising, and patting of serums have been shown to reduce stress and ground us in the present moment. So, quite frankly, if the thought of assembling an outfit feels like advanced geometry, a bold lipstick or a swipe of shimmering eyeshadow can do the heavy lifting. A single brushstroke can shift a mood, a flick of eyeliner can redefine an entire day. It's the beauty of micro-rebellion: tiny, defiant acts of self-celebration. Alternatively, book the facial. Pamper yourself.

Socialising over social media: *Step away from the screen*

Finally, there's social media – the modern-day funhouse mirror, distorting our self-perception with a cocktail of face-tuning sorcery, suspiciously good lighting, and angles that defy both physics and reality. Unsurprisingly, science backs up what we've all felt after a doom-scroll session: social media is a breeding ground for body dissatisfaction (Fardouly et al., 2015). The more we marinate in these curated illusions, the more our brains – those gullible little sponges – start mistaking them for reality (Perloff, 2014). Our ancient wiring compels us to compare, but here's the truth: when the comparison pool consists of digitally enhanced mirages, it's no wonder we feel like we're falling short. Worry not, dear reader, the solution is simple: set boundaries on mindless scrolling. Only welcome those who celebrate real bodies, real joy, and real diversity. And above all, remind yourself that what you see online isn't real life; it's a performance with flattering filters and an exorbitant PR team. And in reality, when all is said and done, the only *glow up* that truly matters is the one that happens when you log out and live.

Mirror, mirror on the wall, I am pretty after all

And so, dear reader, we arrive at the final stitch of this tapestry, the last note in a symphony that has, hopefully, re-orchestrated the way you see yourself. We have unravelled the fabric of body image, examined the societal stitches that have hemmed us in, and, most importantly, tailored new ways to reclaim our reflection. Through science, psychology, and the unshakable power of personal style, we have proven that fashion is not just about covering the body, it is about honouring it. Josie showed us that small changes – tiny revolutions in our daily dress – can build a bridge between self-perception and self-celebration. Willow taught us that transformation is not measured by the inches lost, but by the confidence gained. And you, gorgeous reader, are next. Whether it's through the precision of a perfectly lined lip, the refusal to let a number on a tag dictate your worth, or the most radical choice of all – to finally look in the mirror and meet yourself with kindness, let this be your sign to step forward. No more shame. No more apologising. No more waiting until tomorrow or until you're smaller or smoother or leaner or meaner. Your body has carried you through every joy, every heartbreak, every triumph. It has soared in your success, mended in your sorrow, fluttered at the rush of love, and steadied you when the world felt unkind. It has been your constant, your home, your silent warrior – breathing, beating, persisting. So honour it. Wrap it in silk, drape it in jewels, paint it in colours that make your spirit sing. And from this moment forward, let it exist without apology, without hesitation, without shame – simply as it is, simply as... you.

5
Identifying and illustrating our emotions

Our emotions do not exist in a vacuum, nor do they float through our consciousness like unattached wisps of thought. They are *embodied* – felt in the clench of a jaw, the weight of slumped shoulders, the breath caught high in our chests. Our emotions are the brushstrokes that paint the canvas of our existence, the proof that we are not just existing, but *living*. They amplify our joys, deepen our misery, and charge every memory with meaning. They are the pulse beneath our quiet moments, and the wildfire in our most passionate ones. Without them, life is nothing more than a greyscale sketch: existing in theory, but devoid of the vivid, electric intensity that makes it worthwhile. Emotions, quite frankly, are everything. And with that, I couldn't help but wonder – as one does on a regular Tuesday afternoon: if our emotions reside rent-free in our bodies, prompting our every move, and shaping our very existence, shouldn't we be dressing them too? Shouldn't we be curating our wardrobes with the same intention we give to our thoughts, our moods, and our very sense of self? After all, if we still manage to wear our hearts on our sleeves, why not our joy, our confidence, and our power too?

William James wasn't just your average psychologist; he was *the* psychologist of his time, throwing down theories with the flair of a nineteenth-century mic drop. In *The Principles of Psychology* (1890), he made the rather bold proposition: emotions aren't just felt, they are *lived*. As he put it, "the bodily changes follow directly the perception of the exciting fact, and that our feeling of the same changes as they occur *is* the emotion". Now, in the spirit of keeping this book free of all intimidating jargon and pretentious nonsense, allow me to translate: essentially, emotions stem from your interpretation of your physical sensations – your heart racing would lead you to realise that you're afraid. You have a physiological response – heart beating wildly – to environmental stimuli, and your emotional definition of that physical response is what leads to your emotional experience – fear. Let that sink in and give yourself a moment to bask in the sheer *wow* of it all. This became the foundation of what is now known as the James-Lange Theory of Emotion; one of the earliest – and most debated – explanations for how our emotions work. James and Danish physiologist Carl Lange independently suggested that our emotions don't just magically appear; they are a direct consequence of physiological changes in the body. And in favour of keeping this fun and the furthest thing from a maze of dense theory, I'll elaborate. Happiness: heart racing, face warming, your entire body hums with energy, and *then* your brain registers joy. Sadness: shoulders slumping, breathing slows, and every bone and muscle feels instantly heavier; it's only *then* that your mind confirms the misery. Physiology first, emotions second.

Naturally, not everyone was on board with this chronological shake-up. Walter Cannon and Philip Bard were two of said individuals. They politely, but firmly, threw their arms up in scepticism and respectfully disagreed. The Cannon-Bard theory argued that emotion and arousal happen *simultaneously,* not sequentially. Consider the split second before delivering a toast at an illustrious soirée, crystal flute in hand, the room poised in anticipation. Cannon and Bard would argue that you experience both the emotional thrill and the physiological response in perfect synchrony. No waiting, immediate emotional gratification.

But this? This is the revolutionary part. The revelation that had me both welling up with tears and pirouetting around my room in a euphoria-induced victory dance: Regardless of whether you side with James-Lange – body first, feelings second – or Cannon-Bard – body and feelings together – one thing is clear, physiological changes never come *after* emotions. Your body is either leading the charge or marching in synch with your feelings, but it's never trailing behind. Which means – brace yourself – what happens in the body can dictate what happens in the mind. Feels like discovering fire, doesn't it? So, if we return to James' original assertion, we must ask: if our emotions are born from our bodies, and our bodies are dressed, doesn't that make clothing a co-conspirator in our emotional experience? If posture alone can change our mood what about fabric, fit, and form? Consider this: a sharply tailored blazer doesn't just rest on your shoulders, it pulls them back, lifting your spine, shifting your stance, altering the way you occupy space. A soft, weighted knit doesn't just warm your skin, it grounds you, slows your breath, wraps you in psychological safety. If our bodies are the conduits through which emotion flows, then fashion isn't just aesthetic – it's *active.* It sculpts us, signals to our nervous system, and orchestrates the feelings that follow. And if our bodies precede emotion – if they dictate or synchronise with how we feel – then our clothing, as an extension of the body, becomes a tool of emotional architecture. An emotional exoskeleton, if you will. So the question was never truly about *what* you wear; it's, in reality, about *what you're making yourself feel* by wearing it.

Well, now that we've unravelled the mechanics of emotion, the next logical question presents itself: Why do emotions matter so much? Why should we care about these internal shifts, these biochemical fireworks that dictate our every thought and action? Because, quite simply, they are the architects of our wellbeing. They are not passive, fleeting sensations, but the very foundation upon which our mental and physical health is built. Smith and Yates (2018) underscore this beautifully in their research, revealing that the relationship among our physical bodies, positive body image, and *hedonic pleasure* from dressing plays a fundamental role in maintaining overall wellbeing. And they're not alone – Masuch and Hefferon (2014) found that positive emotions aren't just brief bursts of joy; they are the fuel that powers our very existence. Emotions fortify our physical health, sharpen our minds, and act as the invisible pillars of our wellbeing. And if you've ventured this far into these pages, I assume wellbeing is not just an idle fancy but the equivalent of your very own crown jewels, is it not? I also assume you're now nodding. So, if emotions are the currency of our wellbeing, and we know they can be shaped – no, *orchestrated* – by the body, then fashion is not merely aesthetic, it's instrumental. Our clothing, our second skin, our wearable environment, becomes a tool of emotional mastery. Dressing, therefore, ceases to be a passive routine and instead transforms into a sacred ritual, an unspoken act of self-determination. And with that, perhaps it's time we stop viewing our wardrobes as mere collections of garments and start seeing them for what they truly are: an arsenal of emotional instruments, poised and waiting to be played.

If we were to build on this, to truly grasp the influence and musicality of our emotions, then we must first recognise that they do not play alone. They play in concert with our senses, our memories, and the invisible rhythms that dictate our every interaction with the world. And taking up the conductor's baton in this grand orchestration is the brilliant Wendy Moody, who, in her 2010 exploratory study, masterfully illustrates how our clothing choices shape our emotional states; not just through fabric and fit, but through the intricate interplay of multi-sensory aspects, social factors, and symbolic associations. Symbolic association, for instance, as highlighted in the work of Dr. Karen Pine, reveals that clothing with embedded meaning can trigger long-held memories, stirring emotions we may not even realise are resting beneath the surface. The Welsh Rugby team, for example, has wielded this psychological tool to perfection: each player's shirt was embroidered with a single, powerful word: *calon*. Heart in Welsh. And if you were to take a closer look, you might feel a warm bloom in your chest when you realise that the digits on their jerseys, the ones you might have once dismissed as mere formality, are anything but. They are mosaics – fragments of faces, thousands of devoted fans woven into the very fabric of the game, watching, willing, believing. Those hidden totems are more than mere design choices; they serve as constant reminders of pride, legacy, and the weight of expectation. And, lo and behold, the players' performance reflected it. As if their uniforms were stitched with polyester and superpowers, they charged onto the field carrying the essence of an entire nation, playing with an unshakable sense of purpose. Symbolism couture.

Similarly, there are multi-sensory aspects; the way garments don't just drape the body but direct it, commanding presence before we've even drawn breath. Harvard psychologist Amy Cuddy's research on power posing shattered the notion that confidence is purely internal, proving instead that the way we carry ourselves can reconfigure our very biology. A single minute standing tall – shoulders back, chin lifted, limbs expanded – has been shown to raise testosterone, the confidence hormone, and lower cortisol, the stress hormone. So, naturally, of course, I went about my own little investigation and explored the profound effect that garments, similar to posture, could have in sculpting us into the roles we're desperate to play. I mean, by definition, multi-sensory aspects shape both posture and clothing – just as the act of standing tall in a power pose activates muscles, shifts weight distribution, and sends biofeedback to the brain, the structure of a sharply tailored suit does the same. Allow me a moment to paint you a picture – one, quite frankly, I'd been waiting to share from the start:

The structured shoulders, by fit and design, broaden the frame, sculpting a presence that is both commanding and assured. But their influence does not stop at aesthetics – they extend beyond the seams, urging the wearer to stand taller, to occupy space with the quiet certainty of someone who belongs in the room. The nipped waist, tailored with precision, does more than define the silhouette; it orchestrates a posture of purpose, drawing the body into a stance of balance, control, and intention. And the sleek, deliberate cut. Ah, that is where the magic lies – not merely in the way it falls or folds, but in the way it moves, in the way it coaxes confidence from the wearer like a well-rehearsed sonata, unfolding note by note. If a simple pose, dear reader, can manipulate our emotions, then a meticulously chosen outfit is nothing short of psychological armour, fortifying the spirit, emboldening the mind, and recalibrating the way we exist in this world. A power suit is not just fabric and stitching; it is a state of mind, a silent pact between cloth and consciousness. Now, some might say that this is all rather dramatic, that well-cut jacket could never exert such power. But then tell me this: have you ever seen a person slouch in a truly exceptional suit?

But of course, not all clothing is designed to command attention, not every garment is stitched with the intent to empower or embolden. Some are sewn with quieter intentions, their purpose not to amplify the self but to conceal it. If a well-cut suit is psychological armour, then surely there must exist its equal and opposite – a sartorial shield, perhaps. Just as we have seen clothing wielded as a tool for transformation, it can just as powerfully be used for invisibility. And, naturally, here I am, armed with more fashion facts than a Vogue archive, I bring you: Hefferon's groundbreaking research on camouflaging and catalysing. Camouflaging: the quiet, deliberate art of dressing to disappear. When feeling self-conscious, withdrawn, or emotionally burdened, participants in her study instinctively reached for clothing that would allow them to fade into the periphery. Their clothing choices became protective barriers, not expressions of self but strategies for avoidance, an act of emotional self-preservation through fabric. Hefferon was not alone in this revelation either; Miller and Rowold (1980) similarly found that some individuals use clothing to mitigate social anxiety, curating outfits not for pleasure or power but for psychological refuge. Fashion, as many of us know all too well, can just as easily be a whispered retreat, just as it can be a screaming celebration. But the true power lies in mastery; in knowing when we are dressing with purpose and when we are unknowingly retreating into fabric, slipping into camouflage born not from choice, but from unconscious habit. The key is not to eliminate the instinct to blend in, but to navigate this psychological tightrope with intention, to ensure that when we disappear, it is on our own terms, and not as a quiet surrender to the weight of our emotions.

If camouflaging is the art of dressing to disappear, then catalysing cheerfulness is its dazzling counterpart – the art of dressing to amplify joy. Hefferon's research illuminates the way fashion can do more than mirror our moods; it can sustain, enhance, and provoke them. Clothing, when used with intention, becomes a conduit for positive affect, a wearable mood-booster, a tool of emotional alchemy. Many respondents in her research claimed that 'feeling good' sparked sartorial courage: a bolder silhouette, an unexpected colour palette, and quirky accessories that seemed like utter madness just days before. And therein lies the magic: Hefferon's work demonstrated just how consequential fashion can be, doing more than just echoing confidence, but creating it as well. As the participants in her study revealed, their clothing choices solidified their joy, turning positivity into something tangible, something *lived*. Fashion, then, is a source of hedonic wellbeing, a celebration of extroversion, a visual exclamation point to life itself. So, forgive me, dear reader, when I ask – if clothing holds the power to summon joy, to truly and positively shift our very state of being, then why are we so prone to overlook it in favour of vices that could hurt us rather than heal us? Why reach for crutches when clutches can do so much better?

So, here we are. We have journeyed through the very essence of emotion, unravelled its grip on our wellbeing, and exposed the irrefutable truth – what we feel and what we wear are woven together in an unbreakable thread. Fashion, in reference to our kaleidoscope of emotions, is a mirror, a weapon, a sanctuary, a refuge. A sweater that warms the skin and cocoons the soul. A single, well-placed accessory can resurrect a memory, reignite a forgotten, abandoned self, or whisper a story we didn't even know we were telling. A giggle-inducing t-shirt. And yet, how often do we pretend our clothing choices are purely aesthetic? As if we slip into a dress or coat with the detached precision of an art curator selecting a painting; admiring its cut, its colour, its harmony, without acknowledging the far more visceral forces at play. But psychologist Paul Ekman would roll his eyes in silent outrage. According to his research, a mere 10% of our clothing decisions are driven by looks alone. The other 90% is dictated by context – by the way fabric settles on our skin, by the weather forcing its hand in our layers, by the obligations of the day demanding practicality or poise. And, of course, by mood. How we categorise our dress is shaped by social occasion and function. Lennon (2007) notes participants routinely sorted garments into categories like 'special occasion dress' (Buckley, 1984–85), 'appropriateness for work' (Damhorst et al., 1986), and 'how fashionable the garment is' (Lennon & Clayton, 1992), demonstrating the enduring role of occasion in our sartorial decisions. There's workwear, evening-wear, casual Fridays, and special occasions. But what if, *gasp*, instead of arranging our wardrobes by social context, we arranged them by feeling? What if, *gasp again*, instead of sorting our closets into neat divisions of formal and casual, we curated our garments for happy days and not-so-happy days? For moments that demand fireworks and ferocity, and for those that call for stillness and solace. For the days when each step carries unshakable power, and the nights when we retreat into softness. For ease, for confidence, for grace, and for the joy that refuses to be ignored.

This, dear reader, is where things get truly exciting. We stand at the threshold of understanding fashion's emotional and psychological influence – what lies beyond is truly transformative. And yet, I confess, I simply could not resist indulging in a most decadent, overstuffed "introduction"; bursting at the seams with all the glorious, profoundly rhapsodic, and intellectually intoxicating truths that I have been aching to unveil. When fashion and emotion intertwine with such operatic splendour, restraint simply *will not do*. Next comes a journey into the heart of it all; the way emotions and wellbeing intertwine, and the subtle yet seismic difference between mood illustration and mood enhancement. And, as every great endeavour needs its storytellers, we'll walk alongside real people whose experiences bring theory to life in the most insightful and extraordinary ways. Trust me when I say, this was no more than a delightful amuse-bouche. Read on, and prepare for the main course. It's going to be – *chef's kiss* – délicieux.

Emotional wellbeing

Welcome, one and all, to the great paradox of self-care. We dedicate ourselves – body, mind, and soul – to the pursuit of wellbeing, whilst neglecting the most immediate, tactile, and dare I say, utterly tantalising tool at our disposal: our clothing. We agonise over morning routines, sculpting them with the precision of a Michelin-star pastry chef. We meditate, we journal, we sip our adaptogenic elixirs garnished with jelly supplements, but the simple act of getting dressed is treated as an afterthought, an obligatory autopilot endeavour rather than the psychological intervention it has the potential to be. We pin affirmations to our mirrors, wake at ungodly hours to bathe in the gospel of self-improvement, and drown ourselves in an endless stream of self-help mantras; whispering from our ear-pods, blaring from our car speakers, camouflaged within our kitchen sound-systems. We do it all in the name of wellbeing. And yet, amid this relentless quest for betterment, we forget one glaringly obvious truth: when doing any of the above, we are dressed. Wrapped in silk pyjamas or drowning in our partner's threadbare joggers. Strapped into activewear or shuffling about in the infamous and eternally creased high school tee that made it one more year, again. Now, don't get me wrong, I am a devout disciple of the morning ritual. My days begin with intention, steeped in mindfulness, meditation, and movement. I worship at the altar of skincare, and I adore a good podcast. But I also know, firsthand, that no affirmation, no ice bath, no oils, serums, or meticulously curated journaling prompt can truly land unless I dress for it first. And I do it all in the name of wellbeing.

And if you think this is all just fun and fiction, just me trying to squeeze fashion into whatever wellness trend I can find, allow me to bring in my best bud: science. Science tells us that a mere tweak to your daily attire could serve as a panacea for the modern maladies of anxiety and stress. Fletcher and Pine (2012) discovered that minor wardrobe adjustments led to a staggering 73% reduction in anxiety and an 82% decrease in stress. To put this into perspective, traditional relaxation techniques, while beneficial, often yield more modest improvements. For instance, a systematic review highlighted that yoga interventions reported reductions in both anxiety and depression among participants by 58%. While these practices are commendable, the sartorial approach appears to offer a more immediate and pronounced impact. So, if yoga's off the agenda, by all means, Nama-stay home – just make sure to trade in the sun salutations for structured sets and call it an enlightened modification.

Clothing, it seems, is not merely a reflection of our inner state; it's a tool of intervention, a force capable of sculpting how we feel as much as how we look. Lennon's research affirms this, showing that fashion therapy programmes designed to improve body satisfaction, self-concept, and interpersonal relationships offer fleeting boosts in confidence, yes, but they have also been proven to elevate mood and enhance overall wellbeing. If you're here, if you've made the conscious choice to seek out this book, or if fate – in the form of a well-meaning loved one – has placed it in your hands, then you already know, deep down, that wellbeing is more than a morning ritual, more than affirmations whispered into the abyss, more than green juices and artisanal face mists. Wellbeing is not a singular act, but a symphony of daily choices: deliberate, subconscious, and sartorial. And most of which are dedicated to our emotional health and regulation. And let me be clear: I am not here to dismantle your rituals, nor am I here to make infinite promises through paper. I would never dream of coming between a person and their slushing smoothies or their devotion to mindfulness. No, dear reader, my plea is far simpler, yet infinitely more urgent: by all means, stretch, breathe, lather yourselves in lavender and the promises of tranquillity, but for the love of all things wholesome, dress the part. Let your garments regulate, navigate, and sustain your emotions; let them help you to fully absorb, engage with, and benefit from every intentional act of wellness you commit to.

The art of emotional regulation through fashion

As we continue to meditate at sunrise, sip herbal tea under the moonlight, and recite affirmations with the conviction of a Shakespearean actor, we need to make sure that our emotions are never left unchecked, for if they run wild without direction, then all the self-care in the world is like dressing for a play with no script. Because, make no mistake, emotions steer us. They dictate everything from the weight of a moment to the energy of a day. And if we cannot regulate them, we are at their mercy. This is where emotional self-regulation becomes the unsung hero of wellbeing – the invisible yet indispensable skill that determines whether we are passengers or conductors in our own psychological journey. As Hefferon reminds us, emotional regulation – the ability to guide and shift our emotional states – is one of the most crucial skills in maintaining both psychological and physiological health. A lack of emotional regulation, research suggests, harbours risks for cardiovascular function, while adaptive forms of affective self-regulation have been shown to yield profoundly beneficial effects (Salovey, Mayer & Caruso, 2002). Simply put, the ability to shift one's emotional state isn't just important for mental wellbeing; it has tangible effects on the body too. And yet, while we often turn to music, mindfulness, or movement, Hefferon's work suggests that clothing itself can serve as an efficient, yet tragically overlooked, tool for emotional self-regulation.

If clothing is a tool for regulating emotion, then allow me to introduce one of the most powerful, evocative, and deeply human forces in the realm of wellbeing: nostalgia. A phenomenon so potent, so intricately woven into our sense of self, that it does more than just remind us of the past; it reawakens it. It transports, it soothes, it reshapes the emotional landscape in ways that are as poetic as they are psychological. My absolute favourite fashion psychology tool that I am guilty of holding above all else, and one that I have personally seen reshape the very fabric of our emotional world. So welcome, reader, to nostalgia. What we are about to uncover is nothing short of extraordinary. Well, at least to me it is.

Defined by Sedikides, Wildschut, and Baden (2004) as an "existential exercise in search for identity and meaning", nostalgia is more than a wistful daydream; it is an active, measurable force in psychological wellbeing. It reinforces self-identity, strengthens social bonds, and serves as a bridge between the past and present, offering comfort, warmth, and a sense of belonging. And believe you me when I say: there is no better conduit for nostalgia than clothing. Our wardrobes are living archives, memory banks woven with the very essence of who we are and who we have been. A concert t-shirt is the electric pulse of a night when the world roared in harmony. A perfume-laced scarf is an unbroken thread to a grandparent's embrace, a whisper of warmth from a moment long past. Clothing exists far beyond the four walls of its isolation, it carries within the echoes of our evolution, the remnants of love, adventure, and every exquisite version of ourselves.

But please, do not simply take my word – or rather my sentimental tears – for the sheer, inexplicable power of nostalgia. Science, in all its precision, has done us the courtesy of proving what the heart has always known. To start, our brains, in their intricate complexity, often blur the lines between reality and imagination. Neuroscientific research indicates that the neural pathways activated during vivid imagination closely mirror those engaged during actual experiences. This overlap suggests that our minds can elicit genuine emotional and physiological responses to mere thoughts or memories, as if they were unfolding in real time once more (Gawdat, 2022). Additionally, research from San Francisco State University (2011) found that engaging in nostalgia-inducing activities can elevate self-esteem, foster optimism, dissolve loneliness, and even ignite creativity. And, in what may be the most moving revelation of all, a 2012 study found that individuals placed in cold rooms who reflected on nostalgic memories *physically felt warmer* (Zhou et al., 2012). If ever there were a quantifiable testament to the power of love, of memory, of relationships – surely, this is it. This concept lies at the very core of Associative Learning Theory, which suggests that clothing linked to positive past experiences can summon those very emotions in the present (Masuch & Hefferon). In essence, nostalgic dressing is a masterful act of emotional engineering, a way of harnessing wellbeing through the most immediate tool we own. A superpower, if you will, in regulating, navigating, and channelling our emotions. Utterly brilliant, isn't it?

Bebe had always adored her grandfather. He was the kind of man who filled a room effortlessly, towering in both presence and wisdom, with a collection of impeccably tailored coats that made him look like he belonged in the pages of a history book or on the silver screen. He was a storyteller, a businessman, a man whose very existence felt like a masterclass in dignity. And then, one day, he was gone. Grief is an odd, shapeshifting thing. It lingers in the quiet, in the spaces occupied by laughter, in the scent of aftershave still clinging to an empty chair. And for Bebe, it settled most in the untouched fabrics of his wardrobe. The coats, the blazers, the perfectly pressed shirts – all artefacts of a life well-lived, waiting for purpose beyond mourning. But the truth is, his jackets had always belonged to her in some way. Since she was a little girl, he wrapped her up in them: draping a blazer over her shoulders before they stepped into an important meeting at the family business, an unspoken ritual of confidence passed from one generation to the next. At the movies, he would lean over in the dim of the screen and wordlessly place his coat over her lap, knowing she was always just a little too cold munching away on her cinema snacks. On their walks home from dinner, she would loop her arm through his, warmed not only by his presence but by the familiar weight of his

overcoat encasing her. His jackets were shelter, security, and a quiet declaration that she was protected, cherished, and above all else, his little girl.

One evening, in a moment of longing and defiance, she pulled his navy wool overcoat from the closet. It engulfed her, the sleeves too long, the shoulders too broad. But rather than shrink beneath them, she cinched the waist with a belt, popped the collar in an attempt to add irony to the masculinity of it all, and strutted to the mirror. What stared back was far from a young girl grieving her grandfather; it was a woman morphing into him in the ways that mattered most. She caught glimpses of him in her reflection; his smile flickered in hers, his strength coursed through her stance, and as the fabric of his old blazer wrapped around her frame, she felt it once more – his quiet, unwavering embrace.

That first day, she wore it simply to feel close to him. Next, she reached for one of his old shirts. With his scent still clinging to the fabric, she curled up on the couch, letting nostalgia settle in with the rhythm of the rain and the familiar cadence of their favourite show. Monday, she reached for one of his old blazers – oversized in both fit and ferocity. Now, you should know, Mondays, according to Bebe, had always begun in the same way, with a meeting. All heads of department gathered to report on the past week, to strategise, to debate. And at the helm of it all, always, was her grandfather. He had never missed a meeting. He had always taken his place at the head of the table until now. Now, that seat remained empty, untouched, both in respect and in pain. So when Bebe walked in that morning, she braced for the weight of absence. But what she felt instead was a shift, subtle yet undeniable. The restless hum of grief that had lived beneath her skin for weeks was replaced with something steadier, something quieter. Something that felt distinctly *like him*. As if, in some unspoken way, he had been there just moments before – placing the blazer over her shoulders, steadying her with the same silent encouragement he had offered her so many times before. Wishing her good luck.

For you see, dear reader, neuroscience has already let us in on one of the mind's most extraordinary tricks: it does not merely *remember* the past, it *reanimates* it. The brain, in all its brilliance, does not bother with timestamps when faced with a memory so vivid, so tangible that it could very well be unfolding in the here and now. And so, when Bebe wrapped herself in his coats, her mind did not pause to remind her that this was a different day or year or world, no. As far as her mind, her body, and this moment were concerned, this was *then*. This was the *routine*. The same ritual with the same weighted fabric draped over her shoulders. And so, her body obeyed. The neurons fired as they always had; the muscles shifted into position, the confidence hummed to life, her smile widened. Her mind summoned his presence, wrapped her in it, let it guide her forward in the same certainty he always had.

What began as an act of comfort became a quiet revolution. She repurposed his long coats into dresses, paired his tailored jackets with sharp trousers, and made his wardrobe her own; an inheritance not of wealth, but of resilience. To

Bebe, her new garments were incantations. A psychological superpower, conjuring him at will, as effortlessly and as theatrically as a superhero commands a crowd with the flip of a cape. And maybe, just maybe, as much as a hero transforms from mere mortal to legend, Bebe had done the same. Because on one fateful Monday morning, as she stepped into the room, ready to take her place at the very table where he once held court, the air shifted. His absence was felt, but so was something else, something almost tangible. His colleagues, his partners, the men and women who had once shaken his hand and followed his lead, looked at her. And for a moment, time folded in on itself. A flicker of recognition softened their expressions, as though for just a heartbeat, they saw him standing there too. And then, one of them smiled, eyes brimming with something between admiration and memory, and said: *"Well, look at that…don't you look just like him".* And just like that, Bebe smiled.

Bebe is, in many ways, the perfect embodiment of emotional regulation through clothing. She did not erase her grief, nor did she allow it to consume her. Instead, she harnessed it – transforming sadness to strength, memory to momentum. What initially began as an aching attempt to latch onto the past became something far greater: A hushed act of self-guidance, using the past not as an anchor, but as a lantern, illuminating the path to emotional clarity and wellbeing. This is the unexpected yet profound power of nostalgic dressing; it does not chain us to yesterday, but rather inspires our tomorrows. Which makes all this, dear reader, the very essence of emotional regulation. To recognise emotion, to honour it, and ultimately, to guide it towards wellbeing. Nostalgia, as we've seen, can be wielded like a compass – pointing us towards comfort, confidence, even joy. And so, the next step unfurls before us – a natural evolution, an invitation. We have mastered the quiet art of regulation, of steadying our emotions through dress. But now, we step into something bolder. Now, we move beyond simply managing how we feel – we learn to illustrate it, to reshape it. Like watching a fairy godmother swish her wand, setting off a cascade of transformation. Welcome, reader, to mood illustration.

Bibbidi-Bobbidi-Boo.

Mood illustration

Mood illustration is the art of dressing to align with, sustain, and acknowledge your emotional state. Picture your morning routine: You're up, brushed, stretched and caffeinated. Before contemplating the day's chaos, take a moment to assess your emotional temperature: Are you, perhaps, buzzing with unearned confidence, or maybe you're inexplicably melancholic? Or – this one should resonate with all of us – are you feeling the existential dread only an unanswered email can bring? Well, at the University of Queensland Business School in Australia, Dr. Alastair Tombs conducted research that confirmed what so many of us instinctively know: women, in particular, associate specific clothing with emotional experiences. His research found that clothing choices are not only a form of self-expression but also a tool for managing emotions. Tombs' interviews revealed that women consciously and subconsciously select garments to match, reinforce, or even mask their moods (Hartley, 2015). This ability to match mood with attire serves a purpose far beyond the aesthetic; it is an act of emotional regulation. Dressing according to your current state of mind allows you to stay present, grounded, and self-aware. You are, in essence, granting yourself permission to *feel*. So, if your emotional thermometer on any given morning is comically shattering at a scorching 41.5 degrees of joy and anticipation, then naturally, the only prescription is to craft an outfit that illustrates and sustains that glorious high. After all, why let a mood that radiant settle when your wardrobe can help it soar?

Furthermore, just in case you needed more of a reason to apply this to yourselves, fashion psychology research has long suggested that women are socialised to have a stronger emotional attachment to their clothing than men. Kwon (1991) found that women are more likely to select clothing based on how it makes them feel, rather than simply how it looks. This is why many women – myself included – function as mood rings; choosing outfits that reflect joy, confidence, empowerment, or even vulnerability. So, let the sceptics scoff and call it vanity – what they fail to see is that this is about wellbeing, about emotional fluency, and about dressing as an act of self-preservation. For instance, one of the most fascinating applications of mood illustration is dopamine dressing: the act of wearing something associated with happiness to trigger and embody that very emotion. This practice is adorable, just as it is scientific. Backed by research in neuroscience, dopamine, the neurotransmitter responsible for pleasure and motivation, is released in the ventral tegmental area (VTA) – part of the brain's reward system – and sent to the nucleus accumbens, which acts as the neural interface between motivation and action (Fernández-Espejo, 2000). Now, if you're anything like me and 'neuro' only brings to mind a cast of impossibly attractive, emotionally tormented brain surgeons on an unnecessarily intense medical drama, allow me to cut through the theatrics: what we wear has the power to shape our emotions on a neurological level. And in this case, dopamine dressing is less about bright and brilliant fashion trends and more about neuroscience – happy clothes, happy people.

So, if we now know that certain garments have the power to uplift and stabilise emotions, then why not apply strategy to science – and style. Research suggests that organising your wardrobe with intention – placing your happiness-inducing pieces in an accessible spot, think, *happy hangers* – can make it easier to reach them on days when you need a boost (Moody & Sinha, 2010). Imagine having a dedicated section of your closet filled with pieces that serve as emotional pick-me-ups. Imagine the sheer possibility of it: Your eyes flutter open to the scent of your favourite coffee drifting through the air, rich and familiar, like a gentle promise that today holds something good. From the other room, the unmistakable harmonies of your go-to boy band ease you into wakefulness – not a jarring alarm, but an overture, orchestrating your morning with nostalgia and giddy anticipation. The shower greets you with warmth, washing away the remnants of restless thoughts before they have the chance to take hold. All small but significant acts of self-care. And then, the moment of transformation: your wardrobe slides open, an invitation. A curated selection of joy, draped in fabric and colour, beckons you forward, whispering: *Choose happiness, girl. Choose opportunity. Choose you.* And just like that, before the world has even had a chance to interfere, your day is already made. This, this is what I mean when I say start your day with intention.

If picking up this book is your first step towards mastering mood management and discovering how fashion can elevate your wellbeing, then allow me to introduce you to one of the most effortless yet powerful tools are your disposal: colour. Since the 1990s, researchers have explored Colour-in-Context Theory (Elliot & Maier, 2007), which suggests that colours carry psychological meanings shaped by context, memory, and cultural associations. Studies have shown that colour influences behaviour and mood, often without our awareness. And the research doesn't stop there: Research from Adam and Galinsky (2012) on *enclothed cognition* suggests that colour symbolism in clothing can subconsciously prime us for certain mental states: reds heightening alertness and dominance, blues enhancing calm and cognitive focus (Adam & Galinsky, 2012). Meanwhile, studies by Frank and Gilovich (1988) found that athletes wearing black uniforms exhibited increased aggression, while those in lighter colours were perceived as more approachable. Elliot and Maier (2007) further examined how colour in dress influences social perception, with certain hues eliciting stronger trust, confidence, or even desirability. The science is endless.

Now, reader, if you'll indulge me for a moment: close your eyes and envision a bold, unrelenting red. Almost instantly, you might feel a shift; your heart rate ticks up, your senses sharpen, your body feels primed for action. This isn't just your imagination at play. Research consistently shows that exposure to red stimulates physiological arousal - raising heart rate, blood pressure, and sympathetic nervous system activity (Gerard, 1958; Wilson, 1966). Now, shift your mental canvas to a serene, endless blue. Feel the difference. Your breathing steadies, tension melts away, and a quiet calm takes its place. Studies suggest that blue's association with tranquillity and relaxation is more than a metaphor; its presence has been found to slow the heart rate and induce a sense of peace (Kaya & Epps, 2004). These subconscious reactions to colour underscore its profound influence on our emotions and physiological states. And in fashion, this translates to the concept of dopamine dressing. In fact, individuals who intentionally wear bright, mood-boosting colours report feeling more energised, empowered, and expressive throughout their day (Eckstut & Eckstut, 2013).

For decades, when it comes to colour in fashion, Personal Colour Analysis has reigned supreme: unchallenged, unquestioned, and, quite frankly, unhinged. The notion that colour should be reduced to a rigid, prescriptive system, dictated by the undertones of one's skin rather than the undertones of one's soul, is not only reductive but downright insulting to the vibrancy of human experience. And fashion psychology, of course. Personal Colour Analysis has long attempted to sort individuals into neat little seasonal compartments, as if we were swatches on a paint chart rather than dynamic, emotionally complex beings. The idea is that we are biologically suited to certain colours and should dutifully adhere to them, lest we offend the gods of flattery. What truly baffles me is this: if this theory were so ironclad, how is it that every bride, regardless of season, radiates an otherworldly glow in white? How is it that any human, bathed in the warmth of laughter, outshines even the most "flattering" shade of taupe? It's because colour – like our skin, our bodies, and our entire existence – isn't just physical. It is emotional, psychological, and profoundly personal. If you haven't caught on by now, it seems, all roads lead to *the mind*. And yes, I can already hear the chorus of naysayers, clutching at their Pantone charts, gasping in horror. But then, ladies and gentlemen of the court, how can you dress for a skin tone when that skin tone changes? Blood rushes, emotions flare, sunlight kisses the skin differently from season to season. If our very complexion is in constant conversation with our emotions and environment, then dressing for a fixed undertone is about as practical as mapping constellations in a thunderstorm. A study published in *Frontiers in Psychology* found that emotional changes – stress, excitement, or sadness, for instance – can alter facial blood flow, subtly affecting skin tone (Thorstenson et al., 2017). If the colours that complement us can change with our emotional state, then adhering to a fixed palette based solely on skin tone is, at best, limiting and, at worst, entirely misleading.

And if we are choosing our colours based on the hues of our emotions, and if colour, in turn, shapes those very emotions, then what we have is nothing short of a cycle of colour and control. A feedback loop of feeling and fabric. The gist of the matter is this: instead of confining yourself to a seasonal palette, consider how colour interacts with your memories, your cultural identity, and your personal lexicon of joy. If bright yellow transports you to childhood summers, bathing you in warmth and nostalgia, then that's your *power colour*. If deep emerald steadies your spirit and roots you in strength, then that hue belongs in your arsenal. And slowly, you will start to develop what I like to call: Colour Vitamins; the pigments that nourish, sustain, and elevate you, tailored not by undertones, but by understanding. So, never you mind what an analysis system deems flattering. Because as long as you're happy, everything, absolutely everything, looks posi-tively perfect on you.

And just like that, we ascend: from clothing as a quiet compan-ion to a commanding force. From the shades that steady us to the hues that propel us forward. Welcome to mood enhance-ment – the art of dressing not just in reflection, but in revolution. Welcome to the next evolution of self-styling, where clothing doesn't just match our emotions, it *manifests* them.

Mood enhancement
Dressing to change your mood for the better

We have explored fashion as a mirror, a stabiliser, a tool for hon-ouring the emotional state we wake up in. But now, we take a bold step forward, into the realm of possibility. Into Mood Enhancement, where clothing becomes well beyond just a man-ifestation of the present, but a manifestation of the future. Think of all the times you've heard someone admit that they dress based on mood; it's practically a universal proclamation. From George Costanza smugly declaring that he dresses based on the mood of the day – *morning mist* – which I can only assume is a poetic way of describing a man teetering between misplaced confidence and sheer delusion, to that one friend we all have, whose sartorial identity swings between two extremes: Every-skittle-ever-made or funeral chic. But here's the revelation, the aha-moment that descends like a velvet-curtained stage being drawn back to reveal something truly spectacular: you manipu-late your mood to dress for how you *want* to feel. A simple shift in fabric or fit or hue or shoe can summon and steer any emotion before your first morning chore. Thrilling, isn't it? Think of it like curating a playlist: we'd never lose ourselves to the melancholic ballads when trying to hype ourselves up, nor would we blast those beat-dropping-heart-racing pop remixes when we need to unwind. The same principles apply to clothing. If we're in need of a lift, we'd reach for the colours we associate with energy and the silhouettes that empower. Similarly, if we're anticipating a calm and cuddly afternoon, we'd opt for more muted sets, neutral tones, and softer fabrics. We'd lean into textures and weights that anchor us. Call it your Sartorial Soundtrack: Where every outfit sets the *tone* for the day.

Track 01: Chain reaction, *Diana Ross*

Let's start small, shall we? Small, literally, not figuratively, of course. The art of the focal accessory. Because while some may call an accessory a mere embellishment, an afterthought, or – heaven forbid – optional, we know better. A focal accessory is no idle trinket; it's a charm, a sartorial spell waiting to be cast. More juju than just jewellery. It is the brooch that steadies the heart, the belt that binds scattered thoughts, the heirloom that holds time itself within its delicate clasp. Now, put your pen to paper and prepare for, what may be, the greatest life-hack-cheatsheet of all time. Feeling overwhelmed? Slide on a pair of sunglasses – not merely to shield your eyes from the world but to create an instant boundary between you and the chaos. Exhausted? Wrap yourself in a scarf, let its gentle embrace simulate the comfort of a long-lost lullaby. Feeling unmoored and disconnected? Slip on a ring or a locket, something touched by time, by memory, by love. And should the day spin wildly out of control, fasten a belt around your waist – no ordinary styling choice, mind you, but a symbolic act of reclaiming your power. Mystics would tell you this draws energy towards your *solar plexus chakra*, the very seat of confidence, willpower, and self-mastery. Science might not confirm it, but fashion has been whispering this truth for centuries: cinch the waist, seize the day. Even jewellery, that most decorative of adornments, holds deeper magic. Psychologists call it a *transitional object*; a token that soothes, stabilises, and carries us through life's turbulence. A well-worn pendant, a signet ring passed through generations, a charm bracelet weighted with memories – these are not mere ornaments, oh no. These are talismans of resilience. And when worn with ritualistic devotion, they become quiet guardians, their presence a gentle reminder that we can, indeed, keep going.

Track 02: Relax, take it eady, *MIKA*

Now, if focal accessories serve as totems of comfort, then clothing itself is the full-body incantation; a spell woven from fabric and form to either soothe or stir the senses. Just as dangling earrings can tether you to a memory of resilience, an outfit can dictate the energy you carry throughout the day. But what happens when that energy is frayed, when anxiety hums beneath the surface or sadness casts its long shadow? In those moments, dressing, as challenging as it may be, becomes an act of self-restoration. While instinct may tell us to retreat into oversized silhouettes and shapeless layers, research suggests that what we wear in times of distress can either anchor us or amplify us. Certain garments act as sartorial safety nets, offering tactile reassurance and regulating our nervous system, while others, however unintentionally, reinforce feelings of disarray. As it turns out, just as we can dress to uplift, we can also dress to *unravel*.

And so, we style to steady. Dress to decompress. A delicate dance, a pas de deux as intricate as any composed to Tchaikovsky. While a dishevelled appearance often mirrors a melancholic mood, an obsession with dressing to perfection can be equally telling, fostering an anxiety that unravels the very seams of our wellbeing. The antidote to life's relentless tempo lies within a wardrobe that doesn't just clothe but cocoons; a personal sanctuary stitched together with intention. Consider the liberating escapism found in dressing up. Research shows that outlandish makeups and dress-ups carry a 'tension-releasing dimension' that allows us to momentarily step away from our daily concerns. This sartorial adventure offers respite, a change to inhabit a persona unburdened by the mundane. Similarly, the therapeutic embrace of 'deep touch pressure' – a gentle, consistent squeezing sensation – has been shown to have calming effects. During bouts of low mood, research suggests that form-fitting clothing, such as activewear, compression wear, or even just a fitted tank, can provide this soothing pressure, akin to a wearable weighted blanket. This gentle compression fosters the release of gamma-aminobutyric acid (GABA) neurotransmitters in the brain, inducing a calming and relaxing effect. And yes, these are all tools that I have personally applied to my own life and to the lives of others. As a woman well-acquainted with anxiety – chairwoman, founder, and lifetime member of the Overthinkers' Society – I can personally vouch for this. But if my lived experience isn't evidence enough, consider this: a global survey on the mood-altering effects of clothing found that 42% of respondents felt more relaxed simply by choosing the right outfit. That's nearly half. And in my ever-racing, anxiety-ridden brain, that statistic is nothing short of extraordinary.

Track 03: It feels so good, *sonique*

If clothing has the power to hush an overactive mind and swaddle us in calm, then surely, it must also possess the opposite ability – to electrify, embolden, and lift us higher. And, would you look at that, it does! Intentional dressing, much like a perfectly curated mood-boosting playlist, is designed to hit all the right neurological notes. But here's where it gets interesting – not all happy songs make us feel the same kind of happy. There's the nostalgic ballad that wraps us in warmth, the euphoric dance anthem that crackles like lightning in our veins, and the guilty pleasure bop that dares us to keep still when every fibre of our being wants to jump up and belt the chorus. Happiness, joy, exhilaration, contentment – these aren't just interchangeable synonyms; they are distinct facets of positive affectivity. Or, in scientific terms, different manifestations of our happy hormones.

And now, waltzing in from stage left, bathed in the glow of adoration and ready to sweep you off your feet – ladies and gentlemen, give it up for the ultimate four-piece sensation: Dopamine, Serotonin, Oxytocin, and Endorphins! A boy band so legendary, their hits include *Euphoria on Demand*, *The Power of a Hug*, *Runner's High*, and the timeless classic, *Mood Like Jagger*. The biochemical quarter orchestrating our moods and, as it turns out, our outfit choices. Each plays a distinct role in shaping our emotional landscape, and when applied to fashion, they unveil the profound ways in which clothing truly enhances our well-being. Now, darling, if there's one hormone that knows how to make an entrance, it's dopamine. The undeniable heartthrob of our happy hormone boy band, dopamine is the reckless, wild-card lead singer – the one who sets hearts racing, makes spontaneous declarations of love, and always, *always* leaves us wanting more. Often hailed as the "pleasure molecule," dopamine is the mastermind behind the intoxicating thrill of a first kiss, the dizzying rush of an impulse purchase, and the sheer, unadulterated euphoria of biting into an indulgent, velvety piece of chocolate. It's the rockstar of neurotransmitters – charming, electrifying, and just a *tiny* bit dangerous. Naturally, this restless, high-octane energy manifests in fashion as well. Enter dopamine dressing – the sartorial sugar rush of the style world. Those vibrant hues, those electric prints, that inexplicable urge to drape yourself in sunshine yellow and fuchsia pink just to *feel* something, that's dopamine at work. It's a love affair with the instant gratification of bold, statement-making fashion, the fashion equivalent of a whirlwind romance or a spontaneous shopping spree. But much like the thrill of a new fling or the fleeting high of a sugar crash, its effects can be temporary. That neon green blazer might have felt like a *moment* in the fitting room, but will it stand the test of time? Ah, dopamine, charming us into fashion choices we may or may not regret by morning.

If dopamine is the rockstar setting the stage ablaze, then serotonin is the maestro – the composed, steady-handed conductor who ensures the symphony plays on long after the encore. Ah, serotonin, the *contentment hormone*, the quiet architect of wellbeing, the ever-faithful guardian of long-term happiness. It is the warm glow of a love that has weathered the seasons, the serenity of a moment steeped in presence and mindfulness. If dopamine is the fiery spark, serotonin is the slow-burning hearth; constant, reliable, and inexplicable in its warmth. In fashion, it is, quite simply, the very essence of *serotonin styling* – a philosophy I have devoted my research, my practice, and quite frankly, my life to. This is not about fleeting trends or impulse-driven frills; it is about clothing as an extension of the self, a second skin that nurtures as much as it adorns. It is the soft cashmere that cocoons you in its embrace, the comforting *and* comfortable heels that bolster your confidence without a hint of bravado, the immortal and infallible dress that has seen you through every milestone and triumph. Serotonin styling might not scream for attention; but it hums in perfect harmony with your inner world, offering a wardrobe not just for the body, but for the soul.

Oxytocin, the *love hormone*, the invisible thread that binds us not only to people but to the objects, places, and rituals that make us feel safe, cherished, *home*. It is the reason a well-worn sweater, steeped in the scent of a loved one, feels like an embrace even in their absence. It's why heirloom jewellery carries the weight of generations, whispering stories of those who came before. It is the force behind nostalgic dressing – that uncanny, heart-wrenching pull towards garments infused with memory, connection, and the echoes of laughter long past. Wearing pieces imbued with sentimental value can remind us of love and, almost magically, *reactivate* it – coaxing oxytocin from the depths of our biology like a lullaby that softens the sharp edges of the world.

And then, last but by no means least, we have endorphins – the body's natural euphoria dealers. The unsung heroes of pleasure and resilience, released through laughter, movement, and sensory delight. And yes, dear reader, look at you catching on – even *fashion*. The exhilarating slide of silk against skin, the reassuring weight of a perfectly structured coat, the rhythmic swish of a flowing skirt, these are more than aesthetic experiences; they are microbursts of endorphins, little flickers of chemical joy and magic. And with that, as the curtain falls on our grand sartorial symphony, let us take a moment to revel in the brilliance of our biological quartet. Dopamine may dazzle, serotonin may soothe, oxytocin may tether, and endorphins? They ensure the entire performance ends with a raucous standing ovation. *Thank you, readers, you've been wonderful...and the crowd goes wild.*

While dopamine dressing is the electric thrill of a flirtation – intoxicating, unpredictable, and designed to set your pulse racing – serotonin styling is the steady, unwavering embrace of a love that lingers. It is the difference between a sugar rush and heart-y nourishment, between fleeting excitement and enduring that everlasting contentment. By embracing serotonin styling, we transcend the ephemeral highs of trend-chasing and impulse dressing, anchoring ourselves in a wardrobe that does more than flatter, it fortifies. Research confirms that 40% of people believe certain outfits don't just enhance confidence, they *embolden* it (Young, S.). This is no mere illusion; it's a full-scale neurochemical production, orchestrated by serotonin, the maestro of mood regulation, self-assurance, and that unmistakable buoyancy in your stride (Groov, *Know Your Brain: A Quick Guide to Serotonin*). In fact, more than two-thirds of Brits reported that dressing with intention helped recalibrate their entire day, with 35% confessing that their outfit alone had the power to transform the mundane into something truly unexpected. So, forgive me if I protest – no, *insist* – that this is no longer about fashion. This is transformation. This is *alchemy*. This is the art of making your day, your life, your very existence on this planet infinitely richer, fuller, *better*. You have, at your fingertips, the power to rewire your brain, to sculpt your identity, to shift the very chemistry of your being, all through the choices you make when you get dressed. So, I ask you, not as a psychologist, nor as a scientist, or even as a fashion-enthusiast, but as someone who has seen the evidence stitched into every hem, one question remains: Do you want to be happy? Or do you want to be *really* happy?

But as we ascend into the light, we must first pay our respects to the shadows. Because if fashion has the power to embolden, it also has the unnerving ability to expose when we feel anything *but* powerful. Back in 1991, researcher Kwon unearthed a striking truth: women, far more than men, allow their emotions to steer the wheel of their wardrobes. And the patterns are as predictable as they are poignant. When spirits are low, for instance, the most commonly reached-for item? Jeans. But not the sharp, tailored kind that makes us feel like a gunslinger in a high-stakes western – no, we're talking about the forlorn, sagging-at-the-knees kind, those that tell a story of retreat rather than adventure. In another study, 57% of women admitted that a baggy top was their go-to when feeling down, yet a mere 2% would opt for one when basking in happiness. The psychology here is as revealing as the clothing itself: when confidence dwindles, so too does the inclination to experiment, to engage, to be *seen*. And it doesn't end there. A study of 400 individuals found that stress, anxiety, and depression don't just dim the inner world – they *shrink* it. Interests narrow, curiosity wanes, and unsurprisingly, the wardrobe follows suit. Women experiencing high levels of stress or sadness confessed to neglecting over 90% of their closets, reaching instead for the same predictable, unchallenging garments, day in and day out. Fashion, in these moments, is no longer an act of self-expression but one of self-preservation – a muted whisper of a once-vibrant voice.

But here's the kicker, the grand plot twist, the revelation that should send a ripple of electricity through your very soul: *this cycle is not inevitable.* Fashion's power does not begin and end with mere reflection, it possesses the astonishing ability to *reshape* how we feel. The mirror is a two-way street, and the question isn't whether our mood dictates our clothing, but whether our clothing can, in turn, dictate our mood. The evidence is groundbreaking. Research has shown that stepping outside one's comfort zone, even in the smallest of ways, can spark measurable psychological shifts. In one study, participants who experimented with new styles, unexpected textures, or bolder colours for just two weeks reported a significant rise in life satisfaction and a tangible dip in negative emotions. Simply put: tap into your inner child, play dress up. Dressing up is for anyone who understands that identity is fluid and clothing is transformative. And for those poised to scoff, for the sceptics ready to wave this away as whimsical nonsense, tell that to the 62% of women in a separate study who were *ten times* more likely to reach for a favourite dress when feeling joyful than when feeling low. And here's the part that makes me smirk in slow motion – those 'happy' outfits all had the same formula: well-cut, form-flattering, vibrant, and intentional. In other words, the precise antithesis of the shape-less, uninspired garments associated with low mood. Clothing, here, is momentum. Triggering, dictating emotional waves that cascade through life. It is rebellion against the mundane, a refusal to be held hostage by inertia. To neglect its power is to silence an orchestra when the symphony is just beginning. So, dress not for the rut that chains you, but for the joy that calls you forward, for the confidence that dares you to take up space, for the life that is waiting – vivid, electric, and entirely yours for the taking.

He broke her heart. He shattered her right before another doctor's visit. Of all the audacious heartbreak stories shared in hushed voices over coffee, this one takes the I-can't-believe-it-double-fudge-chocolate-cake. He left her to pick up the pieces on the very same day she had to sit across from another doctor, after another visit, to hear the words every human on this earth fears the most. This should have been the breaking point, this should be *anyone's* breaking point, but to Vivian – Viv to us – this was her turning point.

There was a time when Viv's wardrobe mirrored the weight it carried in her heart. Black on black on black, layers of fabric as armour, concealing both body and soul. In the aftermath of a heartbreak that shattered not just a relationship but her sense of self, she withdrew into the comfort of darkness. Black became her shield, a way to hide, to disappear. "I just needed something to protect me", she admitted. "And black was the thing that felt safe." But safety, she realised, wasn't the same as healing. Her therapist had gently nudged her towards self-discovery, and somewhere along the way,

she found herself opening up to the world of fashion psychology, feeling exposed in a way she never had before. The idea of wearing colour, of inviting attention, felt like a rebellion against the numbness she had wrapped herself in for so long. And yet, she tried. Small steps at first: a navy sweater instead of a black one. Then, a muted floral print. And slowly, the transformation began – not only in her wardrobe, but in her mind. Viv now refers to it as "learning a new language": "One where my clothes weren't just clothes, but a way to tell myself a different story."

Her transformation was, she found out, about so much more than just moving past heartbreak, about treating an illness, about a routine that was as dark as it was draining. Hospital visits. Doctor's offices a familiar backdrop. And on those days, when appointments loomed heavy over her, she realised she had a choice – succumb to the weight of it or show up as the person she wanted to be. Show up as the young woman, healed, healthy, whole, tomorrow. Whenever that tomorrow might be. She used to default to sweats and a t-shirt – the universal uniform of surrender. "I knew I'd walk out angry. Sad and angry," she admitted. "So why bother?" But then, one morning, standing at the crossroads of old habits and a new mindset, she paused. *How do I want to feel?* That day, she chose something different. She traded resignation for olive green pants, a crisp white cropped tee, and a teddy-bear coat that felt like a hug. Regardless of the outcome, everyone needs a hug, right? Burgundy sneakers, laced with delicate flowers, carried her forward – soft yet so strong, delicate yet defiant.

And it worked: "Even the lady next to me at the hospital complimented my outfit," she laughed. "We ended up talking about fashion instead of everything else." Viv was more than heartbroken, more than healing, more than sick, or on the mend, or fighting. She was a woman, beautiful, bright, and brilliant, in her life-defying outfits and her smile that lit up the world. With every passing day, every visit, Viv continued to challenge herself: warm-toned dresses reminded her of autumn walks that made her so happy. A lavender blouse softened the edges of her anxiety. Prints felt playful, whimsical, a reminder that she still had access to buckets of true, unfiltered glee. And she was worth dressing, worth celebrating, worthy of joy.

It was finally time to stop dressing in black and instead start dressing for the light.

Once she began stepping out of the fog, Viv realised she didn't just want fashion to pull her out of the darkness – she wanted it to keep her in the bright, unwavering light. She was, for the first time in a long time, truly *living*. Physically, she was better. Emotionally, she was on the scenic route to closure. She was seeing friends again, stretching her limbs in Pilates, filling her home with the scent of butter and chocolate – her brownies, nothing short of divine. But happiness, she knew, required maintenance. So, she built rituals, small but mighty. A closet curated with "just in case" ensembles, ready for the days when doubt tried to slither back in. A photo journal cataloguing every look that made her feel unstoppable – sun-drenched oranges, electric blues, fabrics that draped over her like whispered affirmations. What started as a personal archive became something more. *A blog.* A digital love letter to the power of getting dressed with intention. The internet devoured it, and before she knew it, it landed her a job in, yes, fashion.

Even her nail polish, once an afterthought, became a barometer for her mood. Deep green when she needed grounding, bright yellow when she felt gorgeous and gutsy. No more looking down at her poised, elegant hands and seeing pain embedded in the cuticles. "We see polished perfection now," she giggled, wiggling her fingers. "It's funny," she mused, tilting her head, "I used to think my clothes had to reflect how I felt. Now, I dress for how I *want* to feel."

Not too long ago, she put on an outfit that will forever be immortalised in this book and her memory. One she never thought she'd wear: a fitted white jacket, pristine and weightless, softer than she ever allowed herself to be. She paired it with flowy trousers in a shade she once feared: soft grey, like the quiet promise of dawn. It was the kind of outfit that made a statement without needing to say a word. She sat in the doctor's office, hands folded, shoulders back, knowing that this moment – this *outfit* – manifested everything she felt, and hoped to feel, inside.

"You're good," the doctor said, a simple sentence, an earth-shattering declaration. She could go on with her life. *Her life.* The one she had spent years too afraid to live, too exhausted to chase. She had never been one for grand displays of emotion, but in that moment, in her white jacket,

her polished nails, her softly tailored armour, she let herself say it.

One quick breath. One seismic shift.

"I'm so happy."

I want to take a moment to pause and honour the brave and brilliant women like Viv who have come forward to share their stories – stories of vulnerability, of strength, of courage, of breathtaking resilience. To those on their journeys, to the doctors, therapists, friends, family, and loved ones who have held their hands along the way. Who loved them. Who cheered them on when they put on an outlandish dress or a shockingly bright t-shirt and saw it as a victory worth celebrating. And for those of you wondering – yes, Viv's ex got exactly what he deserved. More on that at a later date. But to all the brilliant women who want to understand themselves better, let's start small. A baby step, if you will. Did you know that women dress differently throughout their menstrual cycle? Research from Durante, Li, and Haselton shows that as oestrogen levels rise, women are more likely to choose outfits that make them feel attractive and confident, while during lower-hormone phases, they might opt for comfort and ease (Durante, Li, & Haselton, 2008). Take that as your first challenge. Tap into how you're feeling – not just because of your mood, but because of your body, your cycle, your energy. And then? Challenge yourself to dress *up*. Shock yourself. Shock your body. Shock the world. Because, in answer to my previous question, in tribute to all these brilliant women, and most importantly, to *you* – you deserve to be unconditionally, undeniably, dance-like-nobody's-watching *happy*.

6
Targeting goals

There is an undeniable, almost primal, human hunger for purpose. It is the pulse beneath our ambitions, the unseen force behind every leap, every risk, every reinvention. Without goals, we are untethered, drifting through life without an anchor or map. But when we set our sights on something, when we sharpen our focus and channel our energy, our world takes shape. And believe it or not, what we wear has everything to do with how well we navigate that world. Fashion, here, is a weapon of self-belief, a weapon of armour against doubt, a carefully crafted declaration of intent. It has been proven time and time again that the right clothing choices can rewire our self-perception, influence how others see us, and propel us forward with a conviction we may not have otherwise had. The simple act of curating a wardrobe that aligns with our aspirations can streamline decision-making, freeing up cognitive resources for bigger, more important pursuits. All of which have been directly correlated to ticking off tasks, attaining goals, and, most humbling of all, maximising wellbeing through the gratification of unimaginable success.

In my own words, and bold opinion, the 'you-niform' speaks to the psychological power of consistency. A carefully crafted wardrobe is about infinitely more than just looking put-together, it's a tool for reducing decision fatigue. With the average adult making approximately 35,000 decisions per day, each choice chips away at our cognitive reserves. A style you-niform – a wardrobe infused with your lived experiences, colour vitamins, aspirations, and manifestations – becomes the ultimate efficiency hack, freeing up your mental bandwidth for what truly matters: setting and smashing your goals. It allows us to channel our mental energy towards goal-setting rather than outfit indecision. But here's the real magic, your you-niform isn't just about cutting down decision fatigue; it's meticulously designed to optimise your performance in whatever battlefield you choose to figuratively charge into. Need to own the boardroom without stressing over what to wear? Your go-to wrap dress and power heels have already clocked in. Want to make it to spin class and leave every last drop of energy on that bike without fumbling through workout gear at six-bloody-thirty in the morning? A black-on-black set, sleek and battle-ready, awaits. And so, the cycle continues: one less decision, one more victory. John Tierney, co-author of *Willpower: Rediscovering the Greatest Human Strength*, supports this idea, emphasising that successful individuals conserve willpower by establishing effective habits and routines, reducing stress, and boosting productivity. Fashion, when intentional, functions as one such habit.

But beyond habit formation, clothing operates as a vehicle for self-actualisation, the pinnacle of Maslow's hierarchy of needs. As Lennon (2007) highlights, dress motivated by self-actualisation is a reflection of values, beliefs, and the highest version of oneself. When we align our fashion choices with our aspirations, we're not just dressing up; we're dressing towards something, something bigger and brighter. Whether it's career advancements, personal empowerment, growth, healing, or love. And, naturally, in the ruthless arenas of professionalism and leadership, fashion is strategy, power, and persuasion stitched into every seam. It dictates everything from self-perception to external credibility and authority. Research in fashion psychology makes one thing resoundingly clear: those who dress with intention embody the persona they wish to be in any given setting, at any given moment. Self-esteem is elevated, confidence is supercharged, and perceived competence is practically undeniable. Fashion becomes the unspoken language of authority, the quiet force behind every firm handshake and commanding presence. A fast track to professional triumph.

Consider this chapter your sartorial manifesto: a battle cry stitched in ambition, a compass pointing towards the self you are steadily, magnificently becoming. Let the cascade of research ahead be your arsenal, each insight a polished brass button on the power suit of your aspirations. Whether through the art of power dressing, the construction of a signature you-niform, or the meticulous curation of garments that whisper – I'm sorry, *roar* – self-belief, we embark on an exploration of fashion as a formidable ally in goal attainment. Here, we unravel the psychology of ambition, the alchemy of attire, and the ways in which what we wear shapes not just how we are perceived, but how we perceive ourselves. And now, at last, after around thirty-five thousand words of waiting, I say with all the gusto of a woman putting her hair up before conquering the world: *Let's power-suit up.*

Task 01: The fit of fulfilment

Writing a book is an act of faith. It begins with an idea, a nebulous wisp of thought that insists on becoming something tangible. A writer – foolish, determined, or both – commits to bringing that idea to life, knowing full well that the journey will be anything but linear. There will be false starts, plot holes, and the occasional existential crisis. Some days, the words will flow effortlessly; others, they will be pried from the mind like a reluctant confession. And yet, page by page, chapter by chapter, the book takes shape. Setting and pursuing goals is no different. To have a goal is to begin writing a story that does not yet exist, to craft a future that, at first, is only an outline. It is an act of authorship over one's own life – a conscious decision to script a path rather than drift through the pages of existence as a supporting character. The process of working towards a goal, much like drafting a manuscript, is where the real transformation happens.

A book's purpose is not merely to be finished. If that were the case, we would all be satisfied with blank pages bound in a beautiful cover. No, the magic lies in the writing itself – the struggle, the rewrites, the unexpected turns that make the story richer than we first imagined. The same is true for goals. Their purpose is not just to be achieved, but to be pursued. The striving is where the most profound psychological rewards lie. Psychologists have long studied the relationship between goal setting and wellbeing, and findings tell a story as compelling as any novel. When we set goals that align with our deepest values, we give our lives direction, infusing our days with meaning. Research confirms that individuals who engage in goal-setting experience higher levels of psychological wellbeing – not simply because they occasionally revel in the dopamine rush of crossing an item off their list, satisfying as that may be, but because the pursuit itself offers structure, motivation, and a sense of agency (Sheldon, 2001; Emmons, 1999, 2005; Stauner, 2013).

Before we dive into the different types of goals, their attainment, and their inherent dichotomies, we must first explore how they relate to wellbeing, and why this connection is unlike anything we've discussed so far. Within the realm of wellbeing, two constructs emerge: hedonia, the pursuit of pleasure and avoidance of pain, and eudaemonia, the realisation of one's potential through meaningful goal pursuits. Both play distinct roles in shaping our experiences and perceptions of fulfilment. Hedonic wellbeing is associated with the joy and contentment derived from fulfilling desires. Studies indicate that goal achievement is closely tied to increases in hedonic wellbeing (Klug & Maier, 2015; Koestner et al., 2002), reinforcing the idea that success in reaching a goal provides immediate gratification and a boost in life satisfaction. Eudaemonic wellbeing, on the other hand, is linked to pursuing goals that align with one's authentic self. The eudaemonic identity theory suggests that fulfilling identity-based goals leads to increased wellbeing (Thorsteinsen et al., 2018). In this framework, growth and change-oriented goals cultivate eudaemonic wellbeing, while stability goals – such as maintaining secure relationships and personal contentment – correlate with hedonic wellbeing (Luhmann & Hennecke, 2017). McGregor and Little (1998) highlight the dual effect of goals: when we feel efficacy in our ability to reach a goal, we experience pleasure and positive life evaluations – *hedonic wellbeing*. When a goal is integrated within our core identity, we experience a profound sense of meaning – *eudaemonic wellbeing*. This distinction further underscores the importance of aligning goals with personal values and aspirations to ensure sustained fulfilment.

Now, let's get back to dissecting our goals. And no, I don't mean unpacking phrases like "be present" or "move more". I mean, breaking down the fundamental dichotomy between goal pursuit and goal attainment. This dynamic aligns with longitudinal findings showing that wellbeing benefits not only from goal achievement but also from the steady process of goal striving (Brunstein, 1993; Sheldon & Elliot, 1999; Sheldon & Kasser, 1998; Sheldon et al., 2002). These studies demonstrate that increases in participants' wellbeing occurred in proportion to their reported progress towards their goals, both concurrently and prospectively. Meaning: micromoments of success lead to maximising wellbeing. What's more, when we focus on the process rather than the outcome, we engage in what Sheldon and his co-authors describe as the 'bottom-up' model of wellbeing: the accumulation of small, satisfying experiences that reinforce emotional growth. This model suggests that thriving is not about leaps in development but about consistent, intentional steps forward – something that aligns perfectly with the transformative power of dressing the part, using fashion as a means to manifest and embody our goals. Alternatively, the 'top-down' model suggests that goal attainment can create a radical shift in one's self-concept, opening new opportunities, reshaping identity, and fundamentally reforming life's trajectories (Sheldon & Elliot, 1999; Emmons, 1996). Let's readdress our humble writer. Imagine our aspiring author who, rather than waiting for grand moments of inspiration, commits to writing 500 words a day. Over time, these small but consistent wins build momentum, reinforcing their confidence and solidifying their identity as a writer. With each passing day, each word, they climb steadily upward – from the *bottom up* – to their success. Now, picture our treasured writer who finally finishes their book. The moment the manuscript is complete, their self-concept shifts; suddenly, they are, by definition, an author. This transformation unlocks new doors, new opportunities, and a new and profound sense of accomplishment and pride. Whether through small, reinforcing experiences or singular, transformative milestones, goal setting remains a proactive route to wellbeing and personal evolution.

Finally, it's a little more about *how do we get there?* And a little less, *are we there yet?* Structured goal-setting strategies have been empirically validated as a means to enhance wellbeing. Goal pursuit requires a delicate balance between envisioning the future and grounding that vision in actionable steps. Mental contrasting and process simulation provide two methods for self-regulating towards a goal. Mental contrasting first activates the positive fantasy outcome and then shifts focus to identifying obstacles and behaviours necessary to overcome them, therefore inducing an urgency to act (Oettingen et al., 2001). Oh look, it's our favourite aspiring author back again for another example, or seven. They spend many a moment daydreaming about holding their finished book in their hands, seeing it on bookstore shelves, and touring the world sharing their story. But instead of stopping at the fantasy, they mentally contrast it with reality: the long nights of writing, the bouts of self-doubt, and the challenge of staying disciplined. This contrast pushes them to identify obstacles – like procrastination or lack of structure – and strategise ways to overcome them, such as setting strict writing hours or setting up an online group of their nearest and dearest to hold them accountable: *hey guys*. In fashion, this process unfolds in pretty much the same way. We start by envisioning our goal, and focus on the details: how we feel, what we're wearing, and how our clothing completes and complements the picture. But instead of lingering in the fantasy, we contrast it with our current wardrobe, assessing whether our existing style aligns with our aspirations. This realisation becomes a catalyst for action, prompting us to invest in pieces that reinforce our self-image, allowing us to embody – and ultimately achieve – that dream.

Process simulation, in contrast, emphasises the activities and steps required for goal achievement, fostering a sense of control and commitment (Baumeister, Vohs, & Oettingen, 2016; Masicampo & Baumeister, 2013). Ms Writer is back for that one last hurrah, this time rather than focusing on the grand reveal of their book, envisions the daily grind; the quiet mornings spent writing, the research sessions, and the revisions. By mentally simulating the process, she creates a structured roadmap and develops a deep sense of commitment to the work itself rather than just the outcome. This method grounds her in the present, making the goal feel more attainable and less overwhelming. In fashion, we focus solely on the daily habits that build an almost inevitable reality of looking put-together and effortlessly genuine. We visualise planning outfits the night before, learning about different theories and tools, and gradually refine our personal style through small, intentional choices. Slowly, but surely, we create a sense of control and commitment, making the transformation, and the win, equally as achievable. Once again, research show us that goal-directed behaviour is about more than just reaching milestones; it is about crafting a narrative of growth, resilience, and identity. As research suggests, the path to wellbeing is not a champagne-towered book launch but, pun intended, a story – a dynamic interplay of striving, achieving, and evolving, each word, each witty sentence compatible with the next to compose a life well-lived.

Writing a book requires faith in a future where the completed manuscript exists even if the author cannot yet see the final product. Similarly, the pursuit of a goal requires faith in an outcome that is not yet guaranteed. But what is guaranteed is growth. The process of striving towards something, overcoming challenges, revising our approach, and learning as we go. That's what builds resilience, sharpens our skills, and deepens our understanding of ourselves. It is the difference between being a passive reader and an active writer of our own narrative. There is, of course, the moment of completion, the finished novel, the accomplished goal. It is satisfying, exhilarating even. But every author knows the truth: the joy of a book is not just in having written it, but in the writing itself. The same is true of life. We do not exist merely to check off accomplishments like a list of finished chapters. We exist to write, to strive, to shape our stories with intention and passion. And so, as you consider your own ambitions, ask yourself not only what goals you wish to achieve, but what kind of story you want to tell. Because the real magic is never really in the ending; it is in every word, every choice, every step that brings it to life.

Task 02: Dress to impress [yourself]

Clothing, in any context, is a force, a blueprint for behaviour, a direct line to self-belief. Needless to say, we've established that it is an invisible architect, a silent puppeteer, a force both commanding and transformative. The way we dress does infinitely more than just reflect our mindset; it has the ability to sculpt it, mould it, prime it. Enclothed cognition (Adam & Galinsky, 2012) unveils a truth as tantalising as it is undeniable: what we wear doesn't just influence how the world perceives us, it rewires the very framework of our self-perception. But let us not get ahead of ourselves. For now, let us revel in the delicious details of how a shift in perception orchestrates a chain reaction – one that alters behaviour, refines action, and, in doing so, catapults our capabilities to dazzling new heights. Goals become realities, ambitions morph into inevitabilities, and the self we once *aspired* to be stands before us, fully realised. Fashion gives us the unmatched power to move with certainty, make sharper choices, and show up as a version of ourselves that has limitless potential and unwavering self-respect. It's a truly mystical gift that we constantly underestimate. Almost like a superpower we know is there, one that we possess but is still wild and unruly. Actually, speaking of superpowers…

Research conducted by Dr Pine and her colleagues at the University of Hertfordshire put students in a Superman t-shirt and had them complete a Social Comparison Rating Scale and found something remarkable. Those wearing the iconic 'S' on their chest didn't just feel different; they felt *superior*. Their scores on self-perception metrics – confidence, attractiveness, and self-assurance – soared to 72%, significantly outshining those in their regular clothes, who trailed behind at 64%. And just like every superhero movie franchise, there's more. When asked to estimate their own physical strength, the Superman-clad students genuinely believed they could lift heavier objects. They weren't suddenly endowed with Superhuman strength from planet Krypton, nor were they bitten by a mutant insect, but their minds didn't seem to care; the mere act of wearing a garment imbued with power and resilience had altered their perception of their own capabilities. The phenomenon of a simple emblem or symbolic garment isn't exclusive to superhero logos, on the contrary. Think about uniforms. Slipping into a specific outfit extends past practicality, it's about stepping into a role. Athletes put on their jerseys and transform into warriors on the field. Police officers and military personnel suit up, not just for function but for the authority, discipline, and responsibility their uniforms command. Workwear, activewear, loungewear, occasion-wear – each is a category of clothing, yes, but it's also a catalyst, shifting our mindset and moulding our persona to fit any given moment. And, boy oh boy, is the research extensive:

Just as slipping into a superhero t-shirt can summon a surge of confidence, the right attire can rewire our very cognition; *Avenger-worthy skill*. In a 2015 study published in *Social Psychological and Personality Science*, researchers set out to examine the profound impact of clothing on the thought processes of college students. Participants first assessed their own level of formality compared to their peers before completing a behavioural identification form designed to probe the depths of their cognitive approach. The results were nothing short of revelatory. Those who saw themselves as more formally dressed displayed a remarkable ability to engage in abstract thinking; peering beyond the immediate, seeing the world with a strategic, panoramic lens. The most remarkable finding was that this broadened perspective wasn't just a fleeting effect; it was linked to a heightened capacity for long-term goal attainment. In essence, these students weren't merely *wearing* success, they were *thinking* it into existence (Slepian, Ferber, Gold, & Rutchick, 2015). And while the sartorial sorcery of clothing has been well-documented in college students, this phenomenon extends far beyond the ivy-covered walls of academia. In the grand theatre of professional life, what one wears – as we all know a little too well – is a statement of competence, confidence, and control. Kwon (1994) delved into this dynamic, asking participants to imagine themselves in both appropriate and inappropriate workplace attire. By merely envisioning themselves in the *right* clothing evoked feelings of heightened responsibility and competence, as though the very fabric of their garments wove a more capable version of themselves. This theme was then echoed in Rafaeli et al.'s (1997) findings, where employees linked psychological discomfort to inappropriate workwear while associating professional attire with an undeniable boost in social self-confidence. Fast forward a decade, and Adomaitis and Johnson (2005) unearthed similar patterns among flight attendants – those clad in overly casual uniforms (i.e. t-shirts and shorts) reported a disconcerting dip in self-assurance, describing themselves as unprofessional, unconfident, and even embarrassed. Peluchette and Karl (2007) took this inquiry further, investigating the impact of business formal versus casual dress in the workplace. The verdict was, as expected, that formal business attire bestowed an air of authority, trustworthiness, and productivity, while casual dress fostered approachability; an intriguing trade-off between power and warmth (Peluchette & Karl, 2007). And finally, Karl et al. (2013) sealed the deal, with participants reporting peak feelings of competence and authority in business formal or business casual attire, yet experiencing a curious decline in creativity and friendliness when dressed too casually. The science goes on and on and on. The underlying theme, however, is indisputable: across industries, roles, and decades of research, attire greatly impacts how we perceive ourselves. Whether in a corporate boardroom, a bustling airport terminal, or any professional setting, clothing is a psychological toolkit, a resounding declaration of who we *believe* ourselves to be.

So yes, the evidence is undeniable: what we wear shifts our self-perception. But it also primes us for action. A psychological transformation is never merely theoretical; once our beliefs evolve, our behaviours fall obediently into place. And, my darlings, by now you know me well enough to expect that I would never leave you with just the psychology. No, no – I always deliver. Decades of research on self-efficacy confirm that the moment we start believing in our own capabilities, we are far more likely to act accordingly. A robust meta-analysis has shown that individuals with higher self-efficacy – those who truly see themselves as capable – set bolder goals and display remarkable resilience in the face of challenges. When we believe we can, *we do*. And this extends far beyond the realm of abstract motivation: studies have found that self-efficacy directly correlates with goal commitment and follow-through. In other words, the sharper the mental image we craft of ourselves – whether through the lens of clothing, identity, or purpose – the more powerfully we step into that role. And this applies to so much more than just professional aspirations of grand ambitions. Some of us, quite frankly, just want to be healthy and live forever. Or, at the very least, fight like Thor. Same difference. Take workout gear, for instance. The simple act of donning the right activewear can beguile your brain into believing that, yes, you *actually* want to exercise. Deception? Perhaps. But worth it. We've already discussed our colour vitamins, those potent little hues that stir physiological responses, well, here's where things get truly exhilarating. Long-wavelength colours like red and orange are energising beyond compare; they command your autonomic nervous system to rally, sparking energy, arousal, and a higher likelihood of actually moving your limbs. In other words, dress for your inner Jane Fonda and your body may very well comply. The next time motivation wanes, don't just guilt-trip yourself into a workout, trick yourself into one. Squeeze into electrifying activewear, and, trust me, you'll never be 5-6-7-late to a workout again.

And to every superhero, there's a supervillain. And I don't mean to get dramatic – who am I kidding, of course I do – but what I'm saying is that for every positive, there's always a lurking negative. Our clothes can empower us, elevate us, and prime us for greatness, but they can also sabotage us in ways we barely realise. Take, for instance, one of the most infamous studies in the realm of self-objectification. A group of women were asked to try on either swimsuits or sweaters before taking a maths test. Now, one would assume that arithmetic skills aren't affected by attire or aesthetics. The results suggested otherwise: those in swimsuits performed significantly worse than their sweater-clad counterparts. The researchers, including the esteemed Jean M. Twenge, concluded that when women are primed to self-objectify – thanks to a lifetime of internalising the external gaze – it drains their cognitive resources, leaving less mental bandwidth for anything else. In short, their brains were too busy focused on the bikini-bod of it all to focus on equations. In another study, researchers had participants wear designer sunglasses that were described as either authentic or counterfeit. Those who believed they were sporting knock-offs were significantly more likely to cheat on tasks and to perceive *others* as dishonest. Simply put, when we feel like frauds, we act like them. Our clothes can and will construct our identities, whether consciously or not. And as the swimsuit study so cruelly laid bare, sometimes, all that stands between brilliance and blunder is a mere change of attire. All the research, evidence, claims, and witty proclamations come to the same conclusion, the same irrefutable truth: when we are dressed in harmony with who we are and what we believe in, we reclaim our cognitive throne. Circling back to the you-niform – the sartorial symphony that frees our minds from the mundane and channels our energy towards the extraordinary. This is it, in all its lustrous glory.

There has always been a certain mythology to power dressing. It is no mere act of vanity but a declaration, a weapon, a strategy centuries in the making. From the regal robes of monarchs to the carefully tailored suits of Wall Street titans, clothing has long been a tool of silent persuasion, a language spoken before a single word leaves our lips. And yet, for the longest time, the game was not designed with women in mind. But when they arrived – cracking ceilings, breaking barriers, rewriting rules – my goodness, did they dress the part. The 1980s witnessed the birth of the modern power suit; its silhouette sharpened with shoulder pads, sculpted not just for style, but for battle. Women, once relegated to the margins, now carved out their place with structure, strength, and the audacity to take

up space where they had long been dismissed, diminished, or denied. Science even played along: studies showed that broader shoulders projected dominance, mirroring the testosterone-fuelled stature of their male counterparts. And so, women walked into boardrooms clad in structure and strength, wearing their ambition as visibly as a crown.

But – to a certain extent, trying not to get too political here – times have changed. The old boys' clubs are dwindling, and success no longer demands a costume of masculinity. Today, the most powerful thing a woman can wear is her conviction. And that was Phina's greatest garment.

Twenty-five, ambitious, and in love with the art of expression. A brand content manager by title, an artist by nature. For Phina, fashion has never been a frivolity, it has been a mirror, a megaphone, a form of speech more fluent than words. Accessories are her punctuation. Texture, colour, silhouette, the brushstrokes of her self-portrait. Her world is in motion. A life dictated not by a desk, but by photoshoots, scouting trips, impromptu meetings, and creative adventures with clients. There is no script, no predictability, no pause. Only momentum. Only pleasure. And when the stakes are high, when the weight of expectation grows heavy, she barely registers the whispers and voices sneaking in. How they manage to slither past the fortress of chunky headbands, tilt past the little caps and hats, and weave their way through the heirloom gold of grandma's earrings never fails to amaze her. The ones that tell her she's too young, too inexperienced, too much, not enough. The voices that haunt 80% *of us* – a statistic as factual as it is tragic. A chorus of doubt, a symphony of self-sabotage. *Imposter syndrome.*

Phina knows the game. When the world tries to cut her down, she layers *up;* in power, in presence, in outerwear.

She has learned that when words fail her, fashion does not. When confidence wavers, fabric steadies. She has curated a repertoire of pieces that tether her to herself. Her closet is a playground of power, bursting with a spectrum of colours and hues that she knows supercharge both her productivity and her presence. Her wardrobe is elevated, in every sense of the word. Sculptural flatforms that lift her inches above the noise of doubters, towering boots that make small minds shrink even further. Her mighty suit pants, tailored to perfection, crisp as a signed contract, potent as a well-timed mic drop. She pairs them with her vintage Looney Tunes graphic tee, because brilliance should never take itself too seriously. The result perfectly encapsulates her wit, her professionalism, and her audacious sense of humour. All of which, incidentally, she is. And of course, lest we forget, her accessories. Her quiet jingle of power. Rings that flash when she gestures mid-presentation, adding a final, undeniable exclamation point to her workplace manifesto. Or her stack of necklaces that gleam when Phina lifts her chin in power and poise, daring anyone to question who she is, how she got here, or – heaven help us – if she could send the graphic as a JPEG instead of a PNG…

Yes. They already know the answer.

Some days, the goal is grand: land the client, seal the deal, own the damn room. Other days, the goal is something quieter, smaller, perhaps, but existentially more important: just to feel good today. Because the truth, and Phina knows this better than most, is that power dressing isn't about external validation, it's about internal transformation. "If I want to get a client, I dress well. I feel better. I get what I want," she muses, adjusting the cuff of her khaki green shirt. "And if I don't? It doesn't matter. What matters is that I showed up. I showed up for me. And that means I win."

I cannot make this stuff up, reader. I'll send you the transcripts.

I check in with Phina often. I see her floating through the city, weaving between the hustle and honking horns, dressing like a boss or a bouquet of flowers. I see the intentionality behind every fit, the chaos behind every choice, and the irony of it all. I applaud her when she makes waves in the industry with nothing more than brilliance and a blazer. And I learn from her when she admits to the off days. When the voices win. When bureaucracy and hypocrisy take the point. And I love it, most of all, when she does it all with a little sun-embroidered sock peeking from the trim of her trousers.

Task 03: Mind over material?

I teased Enclothed Cognition before, gave you just the barest glimpse of its power, but to leave it at that would be an unforgivable crime against both science and style. No, my darlings, this is not some fleeting concept, some whimsical sartorial footnote in the records of psychology. This is the foundational pillar of fashion psychology, and if I'm being honest, my very reason for being. But before we revel in its revelations, let us first pay our respects to its predecessor: Embodied Cognition. You see, psychology has long held the mistaken belief that cognition is an ivory tower, untouched by the physical world. That thought is thought, and body is body, and never the twain shall meet. But Embodied Cognition tells us, with absolute conviction, that the mind and the body are not merely linked; they are indistinguishable. The way we stand, the way we gesture, the way we physically exist in space; all of it sculpts our cognition in ways we are only beginning to understand. And if the body can alter the mind, then surely, *surely*, what we place upon that body must wield even greater influence. Enter, our most esteemed, Adam and Galinsky (2012). Two researchers who had the audacity to ask if an item of clothing could, fundamentally, alter the way we think. To find out, they orchestrated an experiment of almost theatrical brilliance…

First, they gathered a group of unsuspecting participants and gave them a classic psychological challenge: A task that requires one to identify the colour of a word rather than the word itself. Simple, yet deceptive. But here's where it gets interesting – one group performed the test in their everyday clothes, the other wore a white lab coat, a garment deeply entrenched in our collective psyche as the uniform of precision, intellect, and meticulous care. The group sporting lab coats outperformed their casually dressed counterparts with a level of accuracy that was impossible to ignore. They made fewer mistakes, demonstrated sharper focus – whether consciously or not – and became the identity their clothing suggested. It was as if, the moment they slipped on that coat, they also slipped into a more focused, more diligent, more cognitively enhanced version of themselves. Superheroes have their capes, mortals have their lab coats. Adam and Galinsky gave this phenomenon a name: Enclothed Cognition. The systematic influence that clothes have on the wearer's psychological processes (Adam & Galinksy, 2012).

But our tale does not end there, Adam and Galinsky (2012) did not stop at merely proving that wearing a lab coat had an effect; no, they questioned the narrative of the garment itself as well. So, they split their participants once more. This time, one group was told their white coats were *doctors' coats*, imbued with all the symbolic weight of medical expertise. And the other group was told their coats were *painters' smocks*, associated instead with creativity and free expression. Same coat, different meaning. And yet, once again, the results were profound. The *doctor's* group scored significantly higher on attention-based tasks than those in the *painters'* smocks. It wasn't the fabric, nor was it the fit; it was *the meaning*. The sheer belief in what they were wearing was enough to shape their cognition. This, dearest reader, is the grand crescendo, the pièce de résistance, the very essence of what we've been orchestrating all along. The meaning we stitch into our garments, the stories we drape across our shoulders, wield a power so profound, so utterly transformative, that it bends the contours of our thoughts, rewires the synapses of our psyche, and sculpts the architecture of our behaviour. This isn't about fashion in isolation; it's about fashion in relation to cognition, self-belief, and the alchemy of perception. The right ensemble can summon us into existence, shape our reality, and propel us towards everything we've ever wanted with a force that is nothing short of cathartic, therapeutic, and dare I say – extraordinary.

So, that little paragraph of passion was set off by Adam and Galinsky's (2012) work on self-perception. But wait, there is one final layer to their sartorial sorcery, one that elevates enclothed cognition from a personal phenomenon to a social force. For you see, once their findings were published, enclothed cognition could no longer exist in a vacuum. The world – myself included – began to question clothing beyond self-perception: what about external perceptions, expectations, and reactions? And most importantly, how can we use this to our advantage?

Task 04: Conning couture

Welcome, reader, to the heart and soul of fashion psychology. You've made it this far, there's no turning back now. Beyond the manipulations of self-perception, when we opt for garments with symbolic weight, we alter the very fabric of how the world perceives us. Clothing, after all, is one of the most immediate and potent nonverbal signals we wield. Research on impression formation and social cognition has long confirmed that people make instantaneous judgments about intelligence, competence, and authority based solely on what we wear. Take, for instance, the Pygmalion Effect – a psychological marvel in which high expectations foster heightened performance. If your attire whispers bossy and brilliant, people will, often without realising it, treat you as though you are more knowledgeable, more capable, and more commanding. And here's where it gets truly fascinating: their belief in you seeps into *your* self-perception. Their validation acts as a mirror, reflecting an image of competence so convincing that you begin to believe it yourself. What follows is a dizzying cognitive and social feedback loop, an elegant psychological tango, if you will. Your clothing shifts your self-perception. Your self-perception shifts your behaviour. Your behaviour reshapes how others interact with you. And their interaction twirls, dips, and circles right back, reinforcing the very belief you stepped into when you got dressed.

A study published in the *Clothing and Textiles Research Journal* found that in a classroom setting, both teachers and students assumed that female students wearing shorts and t-shirts were of lower intelligence and scholastic ability compared to their peers who had been strategically dressed in suits by researchers. The phenomenon posed here, that outfits have the ability to not only express expectations, but set them, is incredible. John T. Molloy, the godfather of professional dress codes, quite literally wrote the book on it. His 1975 classic, *Dress for Success*, was the culmination of research on over 15,000 executives, an empirical guide to dressing often misjudged as a lowly style guide. His key findings were that formal wear remains the gold standard, and fifty years later, that truth remains as unshakable as ever (Molloy, 1975). And, yes, Silicon Valley's tech deities would have you believe that formal wear is a relic of the past, dethroned by hoodies and sneakers in their brave new world of disruption. And yet, when the stakes are high, when they're facing congressional hearings, sealing billion-dollar deals, or salvaging their reputations on prime-time television, what do we see? Not a zip-up in sight. Instead, they emerge, almost ceremonially, in razor-sharp bespoke suits and polished, quietly ostentatious footwear. Because, despite their proclamations, formal wear remains the undefeated, undisputed, and eternally iconic emblem of authority.

No tech, no problem. In a fascinating experiment, researchers tested this concept in a therapeutic setting. Counsellors were asked to conduct sessions dressed in varying degrees of formality; ranging from sharp, tailored outfits to casual jeans and t-shirts. Their clients, in response, reported significantly higher reductions in distress when their therapist was dressed formally (McCarthy, 2017). But the power of a well-fitted suit isn't limited to the therapy room. An additional study, conducted online by British psychologists, tested first impressions by presenting over 200 participants with two faceless images: one man in a bespoke suit, the other in an off-the-rack version. Participants had only five seconds to judge his character. And yet, that sliver of time was enough to drastically shift perceptions: those looking at the bespoke suit saw its wearer as more confident, more successful, more adaptable, and notably, better paid (Howlett, Pine, Orakçıoğlu & Fletcher, 2013). This is known as the Halo Effect. This cognitive bias tricks us into believing that one positive attribute, a single polished detail, suggests a whole constellation of other desirable traits and virtues. And if one claims – in their own realm of naiveté – that there is no scientific proof that a perfectly cut lapel sharpens the mind or that a bespoke silhouette guarantees success, their brain, subconsciously, can't decipher the difference. The brain, you see, ever the tireless illusionist, doesn't deal in proof; it deals in programming and impressions. And impressions, as research has shown time and time again, shape reality. Power isn't in the suit alone – fortunate for those whose style leans beyond boardroom battle-gear – but in the strategy. The precision. The harmony of fit, cut, layers, and assembly. These are the silent designers of authority, reinforcing competence, control, and influence before credentials are even considered (Scherbaum & Shepherd, 1987; Rucker, Taber, & Harrison, 1981). And in a world where perception reigns supreme, dressing with intention is no mere aesthetic dalliance. It is power. It is presence. It is the art of self-authorship woven into fabric, as potent as the ancestral armour once worn into battle, as transformative as the spellbinding touch of fairy-tale enchantment, except here, there are no magical creatures to fasten your buttons. No, this is your doing. Your craftsmanship. Your declaration.

The pursuit of the power-suit is not about lapels and linings, nor is it confined to the hushed halls of boardrooms and grand offices. It is the uniform – *your* you-niform. A uniform wielded with clarity, with intention, with the unshakable belief that you are worthy of your every desire. It is identity in motion. A love letter to who you are, a tribute to who you've been, and a beacon for the force of nature you are yet to become.

7
Social unity

Social unity is the binding thread in the fabric of personal and collective identity. It is the final piece of the SUITS anatomy, the closing note in our sartorial symphony – but this is no curtain call. No, this is the triumphant encore, the full-circle revelation where every stitch of self-expression, every contour of bodily aware-ness, every emotionally charged ensemble, and every goal-clad garment come together in one grand, human masterpiece. Each of these elements works in tandem, creating a holistic frame-work for understanding the psychological power of clothing. For you see, fashion was never just about you, darling, it was always about us. About how you, adorned in your carefully curated attire, step out into the world and become a part of something greater. About how your private wardrobe whispers become public dec-larations; signalling, inviting, belonging. Social unity, therefore, is the natural culmination of this journey – where we suddenly grow more acquainted with and more immersed in the powerful dialogue between the self and society. And in this dazzling final act, we realise that even our most solitary fashion choices are merely threads in a far grander weave.

Belonging, the beating heart of social unity, is a fundamental human need. Research consistently highlights the psychological and physiological benefits of feeling connected, of feeling loved.

Studies have shown that a strong sense of belonging is associated with higher self-esteem, increased life satisfaction, and lower levels of stress and depression. One specific study revealed that individuals with a strong sense of belonging exhibit better emotional regulation, greater resilience to adversity, and enhanced psychological wellbeing - with implications for physical health as well (Arslan & Coşkun, 2023). Some researchers argue that belonging is as vital to survival as food and shelter – an emotional nutrient, if you will. Clothing serves as both an indicator and facilitator of belonging; what we wear can nourish belonging or emphasise exclusion, fostering either connection or alienation. It has the ability to signal group membership, convey cultural identity, and foster a sense of inclusion within social circles. Clothing acts as a bridge, enabling individuals to align, communicate, and create a sense of community well before words are ever spoken. They bind us, softly and silently, into unspoken allegiances. This explains the deep emotional attachment to team jerseys, school uniforms, cultural dress, and even unofficial dress codes within friendship groups. Raise your hand if you're tempted to wear pink on Wednesdays. Exactly.

Consider, for instance, the relationship between clothing and social belonging in college students – a microcosm of identity formation. A study by Walton and Cohen (2011) found that fostering a sense of belonging among students led to significant improvements in academic performance, mental health, and overall wellbeing. Similarly, studies suggest that students who aligned their fashion choices with peer groups often report lower levels of loneliness and a greater sense of social cohesion. In essence, blending in through fashion doesn't dilute your individuality; on the contrary, it grants you membership to a tribe that strengthens it. And the social magic of fashion extends well beyond aesthetic harmony and deep into the very fabric of our cognition. Enclothed cognition – reference our psychological costume change – reveals how clothing can influence not only our self-perception but also our interpersonal behaviour. When individuals wear clothing that aligns with their desired social identity, they experience a subtle yet powerful cognitive shift. They are more likely to engage confidently with others, fostering deeper social bonds, reinforcing a sense of belonging and shared purpose. The *we* overtakes the *me*. They stand taller, act bolder, and speak with the collective confidence of the group they rep-resent. Research confirms that individuals who don uniforms or culturally significant attire display greater group cohesion, more cooperative behaviours, and even improved task performance.

And it goes on, ever on, like a perfectly tailored coat with no vis-ible seam. A meta-analysis found that individuals who identify strongly with a particular social group exhibit higher levels of happiness and lower stress markers (Haslam et al., 2014; Steffens et al., 2019). It appears that belonging can – yes, warm hearts and souls like an eternal cuddly embrace – but it can also regulate the nervous system. Fashion, as it happens, plays a starring role in this communal alchemy, transforming mere fabric into social glue. And before you picture this only in terms of traditional social groups, imagine school cliques, work families, or sports teams and let me assure you: it extends far beyond. Fashion unites sub-cultures, fandoms, and even the most niche digital communities with the same intensity. A well-placed patch on a denim jacket can reveal your devotion to a punk ideology; a pastel cardigan can signal you as a card-carrying member of the *cottage-core* commune. And let us not forget the internet; a place where entire micro-tribes form over shared aesthetics – dark academia enthusiasts, I see you in your brooding turtlenecks. Fashion becomes the visual password, the entry ticket to a collective identity. In this way, clothing acts as the semaphore of shared ideologies, the silent signals of solidarity. It's why protest movements adopt uniform colours. Why fandoms coordinate tour outfits. Why entire generations drape themselves in vintage band tees they were simply too *young* to have ever witnessed live. It's a visual shorthand for shared belonging, a means of navigating social structures with the reassuring knowledge that you are part of a larger whole. And the best part reveals itself in the subsequent shift in behaviour: when people feel they belong, they become more resilient, more daring, and more willing to collaborate. They take more risks because they know there's a crowd to catch them if they fall. They push boundaries because they trust they won't be exiled for it. And fashion, in all its fabric-based finesse, is one of the most powerful invitations to the table.

But alas, fashion is a fickle friend; it embraces and excludes with equal flair. Social unity's warmth can quickly turn cold, morphing into social alienation. The same visual cues that foster belonging can also delineate boundaries, keeping some in and others out. Raise your hand again if you've ever felt personally victimised by the "you can't sit with us" movement based solely on your choice of fit. Again, exactly. It's a momentary but jarring exile. More from Haslam (2014, 2019): here, the research highlights how individuals disconnected from social groups – whether through clothing or other markers – report higher levels of anxiety and lower self-esteem. Another heartbreaking study shows that our brains interpret social rejection in the same way they interpret physical pain. Neuroscientists like Eisenberger and Lieberman (2003, 2004) revealed that the anterior cingulate cortex – the area responsible for processing physical pain – also lights up during experiences of social exclusion. In other words, being iced out from the metaphorical lunch table stings just as much as stubbing your toe on t on the way out. In open-toe flats. Sandal-flats. The only difference is that one requires an ice pack, the other a therapy session. The pressure to conform, particularly in environments where fashion dictates social standing, can be emotionally suffocating. Fashion, in its crueller form, becomes the velvet rope separating the *in crowd* from the *out crowd*. And nothing stings quite like being sartorially side-eyed.

Still, despite its power to divide, fashion's true strength lies in its ability to unite. It transcends language, borders, and generations. It connects you to strangers across continents, a shared love for the same sneaker drop, an embellished straw hat that sparks conversation at a festival, or the subtle nod exchanged between women in the same *it* sweater. Fashion is our shared visual vocabulary, a quiet but potent love letter to humanity. Ultimately, this is what makes social unity the perfect, natural conclusion to our journey. What began with self-exploration through clothing inevitably leads to a deeper understanding of where we fit in the world. Through fashion, we seek and find connection. We tell the world who we are, but we also declare that *we are one*. In the end, we are interconnected threads, stitched into the fabric of a collective existence, woven together by the clothes on our backs and the shared humanity in our hearts.

US; putting the *U* in unity

We have established that we are, by design, social creatures. Not merely by preference, but by biological necessity. From the pre-historic fireside circles of our ancestors to the virtual group chats of today, our need for connection is stitched into our very being. It is as essential as oxygen, although admittedly, far harder to come by during an awkward networking event or disastrous first date. And while solitude can occasionally be soothing, chronic disconnection corrodes our wellbeing faster than fast fashion crumbles in a washing machine. In fact, research confirms that social belonging isn't just a warm and fuzzy bonus, it's a pillar of psychological health. It gives us a stable self-concept; affirming that we exist, that we matter, and that someone out there will, in fact, notice if we go missing. Even if it is just the barista who knows your complicated coffee order by heart. But we also know that nothing in this book is ever just emotional; everything is also, somehow, physiological too. When we feel accepted, our bodies flood with oxytocin, the so-called "cuddle hormone", lowering cortisol levels and soothing the nervous system. This chemical cocktail makes us less reactive to stress, more empathetic, and – according to a study in *Evolution and Human Behaviour* – even more likely to be charitable. It's almost as though being around people who accept us makes us better versions of ourselves, turn-ing us into philanthropic softies who all want to come together and collectively save the planet – *in matching t-shirts*.

The intensity and importance of belonging, or as Hefferon (2013) calls it "creating sameness", was never more apparent than dur-ing the life-altering pandemic of 2020. The COVID-19 pandemic had profoundly impacted mental health globally, with loneliness emerging as a significant concern. Social distancing measures and lockdowns, while essential for controlling the virus's spread, led to increased social isolation. In the UK, the percentage of adults experiencing loneliness rose from 5% pre-pandemic to 7.2% by February 2021, equating to approximately 3.7 million individuals. This surge in loneliness was not merely a transient feeling but a serious mental health risk. Research indicated a direct, bidirectional relationship between chronic loneliness and mental health distress, suggesting that loneliness can both contribute to and result from mental health challenges. Moreover, studies identified loneliness, along with prior mental health conditions and stress from social distancing, as significant predictors of psychological distress during the pandemic's first year. The impact of loneliness extended beyond emotional wellbeing; it posed risks comparable to physical health threats. Some studies suggested that chronic loneliness had a detrimental effect on physical health, with implications similar to well-established risk factors. Addressing this issue was crucial, as prolonged isolation could lead to severe health consequences, including depression and anxiety. Incorporating strategies to combat loneliness was essential for promoting overall wellbeing. Fostering meaningful social connections. whether through virtual platforms or safe in-person interactions, helped mitigate feelings of isolation. Communities and organisations played a vital role in supporting individuals, particularly those at higher risk of loneliness, by offering resources and opportunities for engagement. Recognising and addressing loneliness as a critical mental health priority was imperative for recovery and long-term societal wellbeing.

Loneliness, as we've seen, became one of the greatest mental health threats of the pandemic, a silent epidemic that left many of us feeling untethered from the world. It's a painful irony: at a time when we most needed connection, the very act of isolation became a protective measure. But as we've discussed, fashion, too, plays a crucial role in this very social connection. It's the visual language that bridges the gaps between us, even when physical proximity isn't possible. And with that, fashion waltzed back in, the great social equaliser. Clothing is the quickest, most efficient RSVP to the social groups we long to be a part of. Whether through the symbolic shorthand of a graphic tee, the elegance of a tailored outfit, or the quiet defiance of red sneakers in a sea of black brogues, what we wear connects. It invited others to perceive us through the lens of familiarity and intrigue. And when used intentionally, clothing fosters the micro-moments of belonging: from the reassuring smile from the supermarket shelf-filler who recognises your signature coat to the knowing nod from a stranger who shares your subcultural aesthetic, these fleeting exchanges, seemingly minor, add up. Cohn et al. (2009) found that such micro-moments of social interaction significantly contribute to overall wellbeing, enhancing mood and fostering emotional resilience. Fashion holds the anecdotal and biological ability to cultivate belonging; tugging at the primal parts of us that crave membership, love, and acceptance. And that, even when delivered through something as simple as a shared penchant for ballerina flats in a multiverse of sneakers, holds the power to make us feel a little less alone in this chaotic, dazzlingly dressed world.

Fashion; putting the *F* in friendship

If social unity is the champagne, then fashion is the flute; delivering its sparkling magic to the madness. Because as much as we want to believe that we're only ever judged by the content of our character, we are also very much judged by the cut of our coat and the monograms on our shoes. Whether we like it or not, fashion is the visual handshake that precedes every conversation, the nonverbal password that grants us access to social circles, cliques, and communities. It is an unspoken language with infinite dialects; some whispering familiarity, others shouting rebellion. And whether we're conscious of it or not, dear reader, we're all fluent.

The science is clear: what we wear shapes how we are perceived, and how we see and perceive ourselves within the social mosaic. A study by Howlett (2013) demonstrated that individuals dressed in tailored, high-quality clothing were consistently rated as more successful, trustworthy, and confident than their more casually dressed counterparts. As it turns out, this is because in the social theatre of life, clothing is costume, and the right one earns us applause. It reassures others that we belong in the same scene, on the same stage, belting out the same message. But it's also not just about external validation; fashion also primes our internal sense of belonging. Think back to the feeling of slipping into your team jersey on match day, the quiet thrill of allegiance settling on your shoulders. Then, as you board the train to the arena, the magic begins. With every stop, the regularly dressed folk trickle off, replaced by more and more jerseys. Strangers at first, but as the colours multiply, so does the unspoken camaraderie. By the time you're halfway there, you're no longer a scattered collection of commuters, you're a unified front. Chanting in unison, trading smiles with people you've never met but somehow already know. A sea of strangers, made kin by fabric and fervour. Or when you slip into your cultural attire for a family celebration, the familiar fabric brushing against your skin like a homecoming. Suddenly, all those disagreements and misalignments dissolve into yesterday's dust. What remains are the warm, lingering hugs of grandmas and the too-tight squeezes of aunties. Their kisses, slightly too wet, their questions, slightly too invasive – but beneath it all, you know, with unwavering certainty, that you are truly, unquestionably, loved. The physical experience of wearing garments that align with your social identity activates a deeper sense of affiliation. In a fascinating study by Kraus (2019), researchers found that individuals wearing clothing symbolising their cultural heritage reported greater feelings of social cohesion and pride. Simply put: the right outfit makes us feel closer to our people, even if we're miles away.

And then there's the phenomenon of fashion mirroring; where our sartorial choices subtly reflect those of the people we want to connect with. It really isn't coincidental how friendship groups gradually start to dress alike – it's social psychology. The Chameleon Effect, coined by Chartrand and Bargh (1999), revealed that individuals unconsciously mimic behaviours, speech patterns and yes, even clothing choices of those they feel socially connected to. This sartorial syncing strengthens bonds, fostering intimacy and rapport. But, even with you and your bestie showing up in unplanned matching sweaters, nowhere is fashion's unifying power more evident than in subcultures. From the goths of Camden Market to the sneakerheads of Tokyo, clothing is the badge of membership; the visual manifesto of shared values. A 2022 study published in *The Journal of Contemporary Subculture Studies* found that individuals within specific fashion-centric subcultures reported higher levels of social cohesion and group loyalty. For them, style is so much more than a mirrored aesthetic, it's a passport into a chosen family. Consider, for instance, the enduring influence of punk fashion; the spiked hair, safety pins, and distressed leather jackets that were loud and laminating visual declarations of dissent, signalling allegiance to the anti-establishment ethos. Fashion became the social glue that bound them together through shared rebellion; just as sharp, unyielding, and iconic as their studded black chokers. Similarly, contemporary streetwear culture operates as a uniform of urban affiliation; social markers everywhere, codes that communicate belonging to an insider crowd.

However, we've briefly covered how fashion, just as it can unite, it can just as easily divide. Belonging has its price of admission, and in fashion, it's often the price tag itself. The exclusivity of designer labels and limited-edition collaborations can foster both prestige and alienation. Research by McCracken (1986) explored how fashion serves as a form of cultural capital, creating 'in-groups' defined by access and affluence, while simultaneously excluding others. This is the dark side of fashion's social power: while it has the ability to create bonds, it can also reinforce barriers. The pressure to conform to fashion norms, particularly in environments where appearance dictates social standing, can be psychologically damaging. A 2020 study in *The Journal of Fashion Marketing and Management* found that individuals who felt excluded from fashion-based social groups experienced low self-esteem and higher social anxiety. When fashion is used as a gatekeeper, it can become a source of social distress rather than connection. *Boo* to the fashion bullies!

On a more positive note, because this is, after all, a happy book. The rise of digital communities has only expanded fashion's social influence. Platforms of all kinds have transformed style into a currency of connections. Hashtags, communities, followings, and engagement have proven to be more than just aesthetic trends; they are visual markers of belonging to a niche, global collective. Studies show that individuals who engage with online fashion communities report higher feelings of social connection, even without in-person interaction. It is, in my most humble opinion, modern-day tribalism – trading the petticoats for pixels. Fashion, therefore, still reigns supreme as one of the most accessible tools for creating belonging. It allows us to forge micro-connections with strangers at the checkout queue or signal kinship to fellow concertgoers. It makes the unfamiliar familiar, drawing lines of recognition across cultural divides. Ultimately, whether through shared aesthetics, cultural dress, or digital fashion movements, clothing holds a unique power: the ability to stitch us into the fabric of human connection. With every garment we wear, we engage in a silent but significant social dialogue – a language of buttons, hems, patterns, and sneakers that confidently says: *well, hey there, friend.*

Alya stood before her dorm room mirror, the soft hum of the bustling campus just beyond her door. In this foreign land, far from her conservative upbringing, she felt the

weight of uncertainty settle in her chest. Raised in a city where modesty was not just a principle but a rule carved into the fabric of daily life, her wardrobe had always been a silent reflection of this unwavering tradition. Clothes were not merely chosen; they were dictated by her family's values, society's expectations, and an ever-present respect for the rules that governed both her body and her soul. But now, here in this city of vibrant colours, bold statements, and unfamiliar faces, Alya felt like a stranger, a fish out of water, or perhaps more fittingly, a dancer on the wrong stage. She was deeply grateful to her parents, don't get me wrong. They had always placed her education above all else, seeing travel and exposure not just as opportunities, but as crucial building blocks for character. They understood the power of real-world experience over textbook learning and the invaluable treasure of cultural immersion. And so, they let her go. With a heavy heart but unwavering resolve, Alya vowed to carry a piece of home with her, no matter how many miles stretched between her and the life she once knew.

A dancer at heart, Alya had always used movement to speak, her body telling stories words often couldn't express. But as she entered her first dance class at university, she felt a deep disconnect. Her new classmates arrived in sleek leggings, cropped tops, and ballet slippers – utterly at ease, their confidence palpable, a visual representation of the world she yearned to belong to. Alya, however, was clad in a loose sweater, modest leggings, and soft shoes, the kind that spoke of her past. She sat quietly in the back of the room, feeling more like an observer than a participant. And in that moment, dear reader, she felt naked in the most profound sense, not from physical exposure but from the emotional weight of being an outsider.

Alya hadn't yet dared to sign up for the class. She hadn't even mustered the courage to audition, unsure if she truly belonged in a room full of girls who seemed to embody a world she didn't know how to plié into. One evening, as she spoke to her grandmother back home on the phone, Alya, as she often did, sought comfort in her grandmother's wisdom. "Are you dancing?" her grandmother asked with her usual warmth, "Do you like your new friends?" Alya hesitated, her voice faltering. She admitted that she had yet to audition and confessed, with a quiet sorrow, that she felt like the black swan amidst a sea of graceful dancers. Her grandmother, who had dreamed of being an artist herself, responded in a voice both soft and steady: "In dance, my dear, in all forms of art, we all belong." It was a sentiment Alya had grown up hearing, a quiet belief that her grandmother had passed down over generations. Yet, at that moment, those words took root deep within her, pirouetting inside her soul, a quiet, powerful sense of possibility blooming like a dancer in her heart. She promised her grandmother that the very next day, she would audition. And so she did.

The next morning, Alya entered the dance class, her heart racing as if the very rhythm of her life were beating in time with her steps. As the door swung open, the girls, already stretching and warming up, paused, noticing the new face. Alya felt their eyes on her, but it wasn't judgment, it was curiosity. She knew they recognised her, the girl who had watched from afar, eyes wide with awe. Their gaze wasn't invasive; it was simply intrigued, wondering what had brought her here today. But then, as if by instinct, Alya pulled her dance shoes from her bag, and in that simple gesture – a soft rustle of fabric, a quiet movement – something shifted. The room, once filled with distance, seemed to open up and embrace her without a single word. It was a united greeting, as unspoken as it was powerful. The girls sashayed towards her, asking for her name, how long she'd been dancing. They didn't ask where she was from, or what country she had come from, or why her skin was a few shades darker than theirs. They didn't ask what her accent meant or what her life back home had been like. Nothing. Instead, they asked which position she was most comfortable in, if she'd danced before, if she wanted to meet the rest of the group, and, best of all, if she was ready to audition.

And just like that, the invisible barrier – one that had only existed in her mind – vanished. Like the left wing of the set during their rehearsal of *Swan Lake*, but that's another story for another time. They had recognised her, not by her clothes – those sexy oversized pink dance shirts and sexier dark charcoal leggings, as her best friend would later call them – but by the dance in her heart. Alya's ballet slippers, scuffed and worn, became the truest representation of who she was. You see, dear reader, when you're a dancer, regardless of the glitter in your hair or the twinkle in your tutu, all slippers and feet look the same. They are tormented, blistered, and posters of the curse that is plantar fasciitis.

And all of them, each bunion and blister in that dance class, were indistinguishable. Alya soon realised, unspoken as it was, it was a triumph. She belonged.

For the next six years, Alya danced with her crew, choreographing, twirling, leaping, and curtsying in perfect unison. The studio became her home, and the girls, her sisters. They celebrated Alya's birthday with a blush-pink cake. She introduced them to her family when they came to visit. They all attended Alya's graduation party. And even now, eight years later, they still dance. They gather at different studios around the world, as they always have, to commemorate their bond, to celebrate the art that brought them together, and to honour the friendship that continues to bloom. Alya, now a grown woman, looks back on those early days, the ones where she first felt the weight of being an outsider, and smiles. For you see, she now knows. She always belonged. She was, is, and always will be – a ballerina.

8
Final thoughts

And so, dear reader, as we stand at the edge of this final chapter, let us linger for just a moment longer. For if there is one great truth our work together has revealed, it is this: the pursuit of the power-suit does not end with a triumphantly raised glass or a final hurrah. Oh no, it is a lifelong waltz; a rhythm that evolves and grows, heals and celebrates, again and again. It is an expanding universe of interconnection and interdependence; never-ending, always learning, always morphing into an infinitely more beautiful and profound unknown. By now, we've surely all realised that, in truth, it all just comes together: how you express yourself builds your social circle, and your social circle encourages and inspires you to express yourself. We have explored how the external becomes internal; how the colours we place on our bodies gently stir the hues within. The cool navy you drape over your shoulders steadies the storm, and ignites a burst of gold within; a sunbeam of self-assurance warming you from the inside out. And that gold makes you happy. That gold makes you feel free. And with that newfound freedom, goals once distant suddenly seem within reach. And when those goals are met, that golden hue erupts into an effervescent rainbow of glitter and sparkles and all things magically iridescent, caught in the glorious spiral of self-belief. But beneath it all, beyond the polished shoes and practised smiles, there remains the most profound truth of all: the power to truly and unapologetically love oneself. To love the person you are today, the one you once were, and the one you are becoming. To embrace the body you have been blessed with, not despite its so-called imperfections, but because of them. Strength, after all, is not the absence of vulnerability; it is the celebration of it. And just like that – would you believe it – your suits are in order.

As for our work together, let us not mistake this closing for an ending. The pursuit of science continues still. It lives on in the tireless work of scientists and scholars who unravel the mysteries of behaviour and belonging, of selfhood and society. It breathes in the historians who keep the lessons of the past alive, offering us the wisdom of centuries at the turn of a page. It lingers in the designers and artists, the thinkers and dreamers, who dare to drape us in beauty and arm us with meaning. And it lives in you, dearest reader. You, who will continue to experiment, to risk, to play, and to forgive. To reinvent your relationship with your garments and with yourself, and perhaps, dare I say, share your story too, someday. Perhaps, like our very final friend…

She was too young. Far too young to carry so much weight, to bear so much sorrow. Too young to watch the vivid colours of her once-luminous spirit fade into muted, shapeless shadows. It wasn't fair, not for a girl who had once been so wild and free, a walking kaleidoscope of joy. Bright yellow wedge heels clacking rebelliously on quiet pavements. Embroidered, floor-length dresses that swept into every room like they belonged there. Neon pink jeans paired with

a constellation of graphic tees, because she was loud, she was bold, she was fearless.

Until she wasn't.

The world, in its cruel and casual way, began chipping away at her. One jagged fragment at a time. It gnawed at her brightness and wore her down to the threadbare edges of herself. Depression came not as a storm but as a slow, insidious fog, muffling her laughter, dimming her spark. But there were no words for it, not then, not there. She came from a place and a time where mental health was a myth; therapy was for the sick, psychiatry for the doomed. So, instead of speaking, she ran.

Every morning. Every night. Her weak and broken body carried her, over and over, around the track and to the end of the road, just one more time. She ran to forget. She ran to feel. She ran because she didn't know what else to do. Her days became a blur of jeans and faded black tees. She slipped into her mother's sandals because reaching for her own seemed like too much. She wore long black dresses, armour against the world. She disintegrated quietly, but still, she ran. And then, one day, she couldn't.

The sharp, merciless pain in her back struck without warning. A bolt of agony that left her barely able to stand, let alone run. The doctors were clear: emergency surgery. The blood clot pressing against her spine was a cruel manifestation of the weight she had carried for too long. And after, they said, she would never run again. It was as though the universe had taken the pain she had buried, the unwept tears, the swallowed screams, and made it flesh. A dark and demonic knot in her back, forcing her to be as physically broken as she had felt inside. And only then did she finally cry.

The weeks after surgery were a blur of bedridden summers and fragmented days. Excursions to the shower became expeditions. Journeys to the couch were pilgrimages. She commuted from bed to living room and back again, while the golden sun mocked her through the window. And yet, somehow, in the midst of it all, she began to heal. Not just the flesh and bone, but something deeper. Something she had almost lost. She dressed, every morning. She wept in pain as she pulled her neon jeans over tender legs, but she giggled when she paired them with her favourite concert tee. She winced as she buttoned a bright wrap dress for yet another doctor's visit, but she felt herself again when her friends came by, marvelling at the colours she wore as though they, too, could see her coming back to life.

It was then that the curiosity awoke. She began to wonder: if therapy was out of reach and mental health remained a distant, mythical thing, could her clothes be her medicine instead? Could they hold her together when she felt herself falling apart? And so, she read. She devoured every study she could find on fashion and psychology. She lay belly-down on the floor, poring over books and articles, discovering a science that no one had taught her: the science of enclothed cognition, history, colour psychology, all of it. She learned how garments could shape the mind, alter the mood, shift the very way a person carries themselves through the world. She applied for a master's degree. She became determined, not just to heal herself but to become patient zero. To forge a path for every person who had ever stood in the dark and searched for the light switch.

At the end of the summer, she moved to London. A new city, a new chapter. She devoured the science of fashion and psychology; ate it, slept it, dreamed it. She conducted her own research, determined to prove what she already knew in her bones: that what we wear can become part of who we are. And by the end of that year, in the crisp December air, she ran.

The doctors had been wrong. She had retrained her mind to associate black activewear with strength, resilience, and movement. It became her armour, her spell, her battle cry. She walked first. Then jogged. And then, through tears and gasping breaths, she ran. She ran through London parks and along the river. She ran across bridges and through busy, glittering streets. She ran to the finish line of her academic year. She ran to the starting line of her business. She ran for the men and women around the world whom she would go on to help. She ran to share her story, her research, and her purpose.

And so, she ran.

She ran to write this book when the opportunity presented itself.

She ran to tell the world – whoever and wherever they may be – that they are not alone in their pain or their suffering. She is here, telling you, thanking you – for trusting her, for reading, for listening. And she wants you to know this: her story – and yours – does not have to end here, pressed between two covers, or at all. Your story, just like all grand narratives, remains gloriously unfinished. And to the dreamers who dare to dress in their finest attire and run, *really run* into the unknown – the next chapter is yours to write.

References

Adam, H., & Galinsky, A. D. (2012). Enclothed cognition. *Journal of Experimental Social Psychology, 48*(4), 918–925.

Adomaitis, A. D., & Johnson, K. K. P. (2005). Clothing the self: The effect of apparel on self-perceptions of female flight attendants. *Clothing and Textiles Research Journal, 23*(2), 74–86.

Arroyo, A., & Harwood, J. (2012). Exploring the causes and consequences of engaging in fat talk. *Journal of Applied Communication Research, 40*(2), 167–187.

Arslan, G., & Coşkun, M. (2023). The impact of sense of belonging, resilience, time management skills and academic performance on psychologica well-being among university students. *Cogent Education, 10*(1), 2215594. https://doi.org/10.1080/23311 86X.2023.2215594

Barber, E. J. W. (1994). Women's work: The first 20,000 years: Women, *Cloth, and Society in Early Times. W. W.* Norton & Company.

Barnard, M. (1996). *Fashion as communication.* London: Routledge.

Baumeister, R. F., Vohs, K. D., & Oettingen, G. (2016). Pragmatic prospection: How and why people think about the future. *Review of General Psychology, 20*(1), 3–16.

Bell, R., Cardello, A. V., & Schutz, H. G. (2005). Relationship between perceived clothing comfort and exam performance. *Family and Consumer Sciences Research Journal, 33*(4), 308–320.

Bems, D. J. (1972). Self-perception theory. *Psychological Review, 79*(2), 183–200.

Bliss, S. H. (1915). The significance of clothes. *The American Journal of Psychology, 27*(2), 217–226. https://www.jstor.org/stable/1413173

Brunstein, J. C. (1993). Personal goals and subjective well-being: A longitudinal study. *Journal of Personality and Social Psychology*, *65*(5), 1061–1070.

Buckley, J. (1985). Special occasion dress. In S. J. Lennon (Ed.), *Social psychology of dress*. Fairchild Publications.

Chartrand, T. L., & Bargh, J. A. (1999). The chameleon effect: The perception-behavior link and social interaction. *Journal of Personality and Social Psychology*, *76*(6), 893–910. https://doi.org/10.1037/0022-3514.76.6.893

Christiansen, C. (2000). Identity, personal projects and happiness: Self construction in everyday action. *Journal of Occupational Science*, *7*(3), 98–107. https://doi.org/10.1080/14427591.2000.9686472

Cohn, M. A., Fredrickson, B. L., Brown, S. L., Mikels, J. A., & Conway, A. M. (2009). Happiness unpacked: Positive emotions increase life satisfaction by building resilience. *Emotion*, *9*(3), 361–368. https://doi.org/10.1037/a0015952

Damhorst, M. L., Miller, M. W., & Michelman, S. O. (1986). Appropriateness for work. In S. J. Lennon (Ed.), *Social psychology of dress*. Fairchild Publications.

Davis, L. L., & Lennon, S. J. (1985). Self-monitoring, fashion opinion leadership, and attitudes toward clothing. In M. R. Solomon (Ed.), *The psychology of fashion* (pp. 177–182). Lexington, MA: Lexington/D.C. Heath.

Dichter, E. (1964). *Handbook of consumer motivations: The psychology of the world of objects*. McGraw-Hill.

Dichter, E. (1985). Why we dress the way we do. *Fashion Psychology Journal*, *12*(4), 21–35.

Durante, K. M., Li, N. P., & Haselton, M. G. (2008). Changes in women's choice of dress across the ovulatory cycle: Naturalistic and laboratory task-based evidence. *Journal of Personality and Social Psychology, 95*(1), 155–160.

Eckstut, J., & Eckstut, A. (2013). *The secret language of color: Science, nature, history, culture, beauty of red, orange, yellow, green, blue, & violet.* Black Dog & Leventhal Publishers.

Eicher, J. B. (1992). Dress and identity. *Clothing and Textiles Research Journal, 10*(4), pp.1–8.

Eicher, J. B., & Roach-Higgins, M. E. (1992). Definition and classification of dress: Implications for analysis of gender roles. In R. Barnes & J. B. Eicher (Eds.), *Dress and gender: Making and meaning* (pp. 8–28). Berg.

Eisenberger, N. I., & Lieberman, M. D. (2004). Why rejection hurts: A common neural alarm system for physical and social pain. *Trends in Cognitive Sciences, 8*(7), 294–300. https://doi.org/10.1016/j.tics.2004.05.010

Eisenberger, N. I., Lieberman, M. D., & Williams, K. D. (2003). Does rejection hurt? An fMRI study of social exclusion. *Science, 302*(5643), 290–292. https://doi.org/10.1126/science.1089134

Elliot, A. J., & Maier, M. A. (2007). Colour-in-context theory. *Current Directions in Psychological Science, 16*(5), 250–254. https://doi.org/10.1111/j.1467-8721.2007.00514.x

Emmons, R. A. (1996). Striving and feeling: Personal goals and subjective well-being. *Journal of Personality and Social Psychology, 71*(6), 1250–1265.

Emmons, R. A. (1999). *The psychology of ultimate concerns: Motivation and spirituality in personality.* New York: Guilford.

Emmons, R. A. (2005). Striving for the sacred: Personal goals, life meaning, and religion. *Journal of Social Issues, 61*(4), 731–745.

Entwistle, J. (2000). *The fashioned body: Fashion, dress, and modern social theory.* Polity Press.

Fardouly, J., Diedrichs, P. C., Vartanian, L. R., & Halliwell, E. (2015). Social comparisons on social media: The impact of Facebook on young women's body image concerns and mood. *Body Image*, *13*, 38–45.

Fernández-Espejo, E. (2000). ¿Cómo funciona el nucleus accumbens? [How does the nucleus accumbens function?]. *Revista de Neurología*, *30*(9), 845–849. https://doi.org/10.33588/rn.3009.99617

Fletcher, B., & Pine, K. J. (2012). *Flex: Do something different*. University of Hertfordshire Press.

Frank, M. G., & Gilovich, T. (1988). The dark side of self- and social perception: Black uniforms and aggression in professional sports. *Journal of Personality and Social Psychology*, *54*(1), 74–85. https://doi.org/10.1037/0022-3514.54.1.74

Gawdat, M. (2022, July 4). That little voice in your head: Adjust the code that runs your brain. PlanSpace. Retrieved from https://planspace.org/20220704-that_little_voice_in_your_head_by_gawdat/

Gerard, R. W. (1958). The effects of red and blue light on arterial pressures, respiratory movements, and eye blink reflexes. *American Journal of Physiology*, 192, 85–88.

Goleman, D. (1996). *Emotional intelligence: Why it can matter more than IQ*, New York: Bentham Books.

Gorden, W. I., & Infante, D. A. (1987). Communicator style and fashion innovativeness. *Journal of Business Communication*, *24*(2), 27–35. https://doi.org/10.1177/002194368702400203

Guy, A., & Banim, M. (2000). Personal collections: Women's clothing use and identity. *Journal of Gender Studies*, *9*(3), 313–327.

Hartley, J. (2015, June 15). How your clothes can affect – and improve – your mood. Stuff. Retrieved February 27, 2022, from https://www.stuff.co.nz/life-style/fashion/69246938/how-your-clothes-can-affect–and-improve–your-mood

Haslam, S. A., Jetten, J., Cruwys, T., Dingle, G., & Haslam, C. (2014). *The new psychology of health: Unlocking the social cure*. Routledge.

Hefferon, K. (2013). Bringing back the body into positive psychology: The theory of corporeal posttraumatic growth in breast cancer survivorship. *Psychology*, 3(12A), 1238–1242. https://doi.org/10.4236/psych.2012.312A181

Hefferon, K., & Boniwell, I. (2011). *Positive psychology: Theory, research and applications*. New York: McGraw-Hill.

Howlett, N., Pine, K. J., Orakçıoğlu, İ., & Fletcher, B. C. (2013). The influence of clothing on first impressions: Rapid and positive responses to minor changes in male attire. *Journal of Fashion Marketing and Management*, *17*(1), 38–48.

James, W. (1890). *The principles of psychology* (2 vols.). Dover Publications. (Original work published 1890).

Johnson, K. K. P., Lennon, S. J., & Rudd, N. A. (2014). Dress and identity. In: *The social psychology of dress* (2nd ed., pp.45–78). Bloomsbury.

Karl, K. A., Hall, L. M., & Peluchette, J. V. (2013). City employee perceptions of the impact of dress and appearance: You are what you wear. *Public Personnel Management*, *42*(3), 452–470.

Kaya, N., & Epps, H. H. (2004). Color-emotion associations: Past experience and personal preference. *College Student Journal*, *38*(3), 396–405.

Klug, H. J. P., & Maier, G. W. (2015). Linking goal progress and subjective well-being: A meta-analysis. *Journal of Happiness Studies*, *16*(1), 37–65. https://doi.org/10.1007/s10902-013-9493-0

Knapp, M. L. (1972). *Nonverbal communication in human interaction*. Holt, Rinehart, and Winston.

Koestner, R., Lekes, N., Powers, T. A., & Chicoine, E. (2002). Attaining personal goals: Self-concordance plus implementation intentions equals success. *Journal of Personality and Social Psychology, 83*(1), 231–244.

Kraus, M. W., Piff, P. K., & Keltner, D. (2019). Social class, sense of control, and social explanation. *Journal of Personality and Social Psychology, 116*(4), 692–714.

Kwon, Y. H. (1994). The influence of appropriateness of dress and gender on the self-perception of occupational attributes. *Clothing and Textiles Research Journal, 12*(3), 33–39.

Kwon, Y. H. (1991). The influence of the perception of mood and self-consciousness on the selection of clothing. *Clothing and Textiles Research Journal, 9*(4), 41–46. https://doi.org/10.1177/0887302X9100900406

Lee, S. E., Lee, Y., & Yoo, J. (2020). Understanding the fashion therapy experience through the cognitive behavioral perspective on body image. *International Journal of Costume and Fashion, 20*(2), 1–10. https://doi.org/10.7233/ijcf.2020.20.2.001

Lennon, S. J. (2007). *Social psychology of dress* (1st ed.). Fairchild Publications.

Lennon, S. J. (2017). Clothing as communication: Uniqueness vs. conformity. *Fashion Theory, 21*(3), 223–240.

Lennon, S. J., & Clayton, C. M. (1992). How fashionable the garment is. In S. J. Lennon (Ed.), *Dress & identity*. Fairchild Books.

Lennon, S. J., & Davis, L. L. (1989). Clothing and human behavior from a social cognitive framework. Part I: Theoretical perspectives. *Clothing and Textiles Research Journal, 7*(4), 41–48. https://doi.org/10.1177/0887302X8900700406

Lennon, S. J., Johnson, K. K. P., & Rudd, N. A. (2017). *Social psychology of dress*. Fairchild Books.

Luhmann, M., & Hennecke, M. (2017). The motivational benefits of thinking about the future: Expectancy and value enhance self-regulation. *Advances in Motivation Science, 4*, 143–177.

Masicampo, E. J., & Baumeister, R. F. (2013). Conscious thought does not guide moment-to-moment actions – it serves social and cultural functions. *Frontiers in Psychology, 4*, 478.

Masuch, C. -S. & Hefferon, K. (2014). Understanding the links between positive psychology and fashion: A grounded theory analysis. *International Journal of Fashion Studies, 1*(2), 227–246. https://doi.org/10.1386/ fs.1.2.227_1

McCarthy, M. (2017). *A psychotherapeutic exploration of the impact of the therapist's clothing in the room.* Dublin Business School, School of Arts.

McCracken, G. (1986). Culture and consumption: A theoretical account of the structure and movement of the cultural meaning of consumer goods. *Journal of Consumer Research, 13*(1), 71–84. https://doi.org/10.1086/209048

McGregor, I., & Little, B. R. (1998). Personal projects, happiness, and meaning: On doing well and being yourself. *Journal of Personality and Social Psychology, 74*(2), 494–512. https://doi.org/10.1037/0022-3514.74.2.494

Mental Health Foundation. (2019). Body image: How we think and feel about our bodies [Survey report]. Mental Health Foundation. https://www.mentalhealth.org.uk

Miller, F. G., & Rowold, K. L. (1980). Attire, sex-roles, and responses to requests for directions. *Psychological Reports, 47*, 651–662

Molloy, J. T. (1975). *Dress for success.* Warner Books.

Moody, W., Kinderman. P., & Sinha, P. (2010). An exploratory study: Relationships between trying on clothing, mood, emotion, personality and clothing preference. *Journal of Fashion Marketing and Management, 14*(1), 161–179. https://doi.org/10.1108/13612021011025483

Nystrom, P. H. (1928). *Economics of fashion*. Ronald Press.

Oettingen, G., Pak, H. J., & Schnetter, K. (2001). Self-regulation of goal setting: Turning free fantasies about the future into binding goals. *Journal of Personality and Social Psychology, 80*(5), 736–753.

Ogle, J. P., Tyner, K. E., & Schofield-Tomschin, S. (2013). The role of maternity dress consumption in shaping the self and identity during the liminal transition of pregnancy. *Journal of Consumer Culture, 13*(2), 119–139. https://doi.org/10.1177/146954051 3480161

Ogle, J. P., Tyner, K. E., & Schofield-Tomschin, S. (2013). Clothing during life transitions: The case of pregnancy. *Textile Research Journal, 81*(3), 252–264.

Peluchette, J. V., & Karl, K. A. (2007). The impact of workplace attire on employee self-perceptions. *Human Resource Development Quarterly, 18*(3), 345–360.

Perloff, R. M. (2014). Social media effects on young women's body image concerns: Theoretical perspectives and an agenda for research. *Sex Roles, 71*(11), 363–377.

Rafaeli, A., Dutton, J. E., Harquail, C. V., & Mackie-Lewis, S. (1997). Navigating by attire: The use of dress by female administrative employees. *Academy of Management Journal, 40*(1), 9–45.

Robinson, D. E. (1958). Fashion theory and product design. *The Journal of Home Economics, 50*(4), 293–299.

Rucker, M., Taber, D., & Harrison, A. (1981). The effect of clothing variation on first impression of female job applicants: What to wear when. *Social Behavior and Personality, 9*(1), 54–64.

Salovey, P., Mayer, J. D., & Caruso, D. R. (2002). The positive psychology of emotional intelligence. In C. R. Snyder & S. J. Lopez (Eds.), *Handbook of positive psychology* (pp. 159–171). Oxford University Press.

San Francisco State University. (2011, November 11). Seeking happiness? Remember the good times, forget the regrets. *ScienceDaily*. https://www.sciencedaily.com/releases/2011/11/111110103303.htm

Scherbaum, C. J., & Shepherd, D. H. (1987). Dressing for success: Effects of color and layering on perceptions of women in business. *Sex Roles, 16*(4), 391–399. https://doi.org/10.1007/BF00289550

Schurrer, M. (2019). How to reframe negative self-talk around body image. HealthyPlace. https://www.healthyplace.com/blogs/buildingselfesteem/2019/12/how-to-reframe-negative-self-talk-around-body-image

Sedikides, C., Wildschut, R., & Baden, D. (2004). Nostalgia: Conceptual issues and existential functions. In J. Greenberg, S. Koole, & T. Pyszczynski (Eds.), *Handbook of experimental existential psychology* (pp. 200–214). Guilford Press.

Sheldon, K. M. (2001). The self-concordance model of healthy goal striving: When personal goals correctly represent the person. *Advances in Motivation and Achievement, 12*, 1–49.

Sheldon, K. M., & Elliot, A. J. (1999). Goal striving, need satisfaction, and longitudinal well-being: The self-concordance model. *Journal of Personality and Social Psychology, 76*(3), 482–497.

Sheldon, K. M., & Kasser, T. (1998). Pursuing personal goals: Skills enable progress, but not all progress is beneficial. *Personality and Social Psychology Bulletin, 24*(12), 1319–1331.

Sheldon, K. M., Ryan, R. M., Deci, E. L., & Kasser, T. (2002). The independent effects of goal contents and motives on well-being: It's both what you pursue and why you pursue it. *Personality and Social Psychology Bulletin. 28*(4), 475–486.

Simmel, G. (1904). Fashion. *International Quarterly, 10*(1), 130–155.

Simmel, G. (1957 [1905]). 'Fashion'. *The American Journal of Sociology, 62*(6), 541–558.

Slade, P. D. (1994). What is body image?. *Behaviour Research and Therapy, 32*(5), 497–502.

Slepian, M. L., Ferber, S. N., Gold, J. M., & Rutchick, A. M. (2015). The cognitive consequences of formal clothing. *Social Psychological and Personality Science, 6*(6), 661–668.

Smith, R., & Yates, J. (2018). Flourishing fashion: An interpretive phenomenological analysis of the experience of wearing a happy outfit. *Fashion Studies, 1*(1), 1–39. https://doi.org/10.38055/FS010105

Solomon, M. R. (1985). *The psychology of fashion*. Lexington Books.

Sproles, G. B. (1979). *Fashion: Consumer behavior toward dress*. Burgess Publishing Company.

Stauner, N. (2013). Goal progress and well-being: A meta-analysis. *Motivation and Emotion, 37*(4), 493–503.

Steffens, N. K., Haslam, C., Jetten, J., Postmes, T., & Van Dick, R. (2019). Social identification–building interventions to improve health and well-being: A systematic review and meta-analysis. *Health Psychology Review, 13*(1), 92–114. https://doi.org/10.1080/17437199.2018.1561412

Stone, G. P. (1962). Appearance and the self. In: A. M. Rose (Ed.), *Human behavior and social processes: An interactionist approach* (pp.86–118). Houghton Mifflin.

Swami, V., Frederick, D., Aavik, T., Alcalay, L., Allik, J., Anderson, D., ... & Zivcic-Becirevic, I. (2010). The attractive female body weight and female body dissatisfaction in 26 countries across 10 world regions: Results of the International Body Project I. *Personality and Social Psychology Bulletin, 36*(3), 309–325. https://doi.org/10.1177/0146167209359702

Thorsteinsen, K., Vittersø, J., & Røysamb, E. (2018). Sustaining life satisfaction through self-concordant goal selection: The self-determination perspective. *Journal of Happiness Studies, 19*(5), 1371–1382.

Thorstenson, C. A., Pazda, A. D., Young, S. G., & Elliot, A. J. (2017). The role of facial coloration in emotion communication. *Emotion*, *17*(5), 678–684. https://doi.org/10.1037/emo0000485

Tiggemann, M., Polivy, J., & Hargreaves, D. (2009). The processing of thin ideals in fashion magazines: A source of social comparison or fantasy?. *Journal of Social and Clinical Psychology*, *28*(1), 73–93.

Walton, G. M., & Cohen, G. L. (2011). A brief social-belonging intervention improves academic and health outcomes of minority students. *Science*, 331(6023), 1447–1451. https://doi.org/10.1126/science.1198364

Wilson, M. (1966). The effect of red and green on GSR and visual arousal. *Journal of General Psychology*, *75*, 103–111.

Zhou, X., Wildschut, T., Sedikides, C., Chen, X., & Vingerhoets, A. J. J. M. (2012). Heartwarming memories: Nostalgia maintains physiological comfort. *Emotion*, *12*(4), 678–684. https://doi.org/10.1037/a0027236

Recommended assignments

S – Self-Expression
ASSIGNMENT *HERE'S TO THE WOMAN*

Reflect on three versions of yourself through the lens of style:

- **The Woman I Am Most of the Time**: Describe her. What is she wearing? How does she move through the world? Which pieces in your wardrobe reflect her?

- **The Woman I Fear to Be**: Who is she? What is she wearing that reflects shame, shrinking, or stalling? Why do these clothes make you uncomfortable?

- **The Woman I Hope to Be**: Imagine her fully – her look, her posture, her surroundings. Break down her outfit in detail.

Then:

- Select garments that represent the "Now" and "Hopeful" versions. Curate outfits that blend the two.

- Pack away or donate pieces tied to the "Fear" identity – create a *Letting Go Box* as a symbolic release.

This task helps integrate your evolving self-concept through expressive, intentional styling.

U – Understanding the Body
ASSIGNMENT *DEAR BODY,*

Write a love letter to your body. Begin by naming the features you admire – the curve of your hip, the texture of your skin, the strength of your back. Then, list five things your body has done for you: carried you, healed you, grounded you, etc.

Follow up with:

- A gratitude list for the ways your body shows up, even when you haven't always been kind to it.
- A social media cleanse: unfollow any accounts that trigger comparison, shame, or negativity. Replace them with ones that champion body neutrality, diversity, and authenticity.

Science says: Practicing gratitude has been shown to increase psychological resilience and improve self-esteem (Emmons & McCullough, 2003).

I – Identifying & Illustrating Our Emotions
ASSIGNMENT *THE CLOSET CHRONICLES: A FASHION & FEELINGS MEMOIR*

Keep a daily log for 7–14 days tracking:

- What you wore
- Why you chose it
- How you felt before and after wearing it
- What emotion or memory is tied to that outfit

Choose one deeply emotional piece and document its back-story. Where did it come from? What moment in your life does it carry? What emotions does it evoke?

Compile your journal entries and memory into a visual or written mini-memoir – *The Closet Chronicles* – to explore the emotional weight and expression embedded in your wardrobe.

T – Targeting Goals
ASSIGNMENT *YOUR FUTURE IN FASHION*

Visualise a goal you deeply desire – a promotion, a home, a love story, a book launch (!!). Imagine it in full colour. Then answer:

- What are you wearing in that moment?
- How do those clothes make you feel?
- What do they symbolise?

Create a visual board or digital collage of the different outfits and write a breakdown of how it reflects the version of you who *has already arrived*. Integrate different aspects of those outfits in your everyday life and let them function as stepping stones to your big hurrah!

Research shows that mental rehearsal and visualisation can enhance performance and motivation (Taylor et al., 1998).

S – Social Unity
ASSIGNMENT *THE SOCIAL STITCH: WEAVING MEMORY INTO MEANING*

Reflect on the garments tied to your happiest **social** memories:

- A wedding dance dress
- A hoodie from your best friend
- The blazer worn to your first job interview

Write down the story of that memory and emotion attached to it.

Dedicate a section of your closet to these "Social Stitch" items – a memory corner, an anchor to joy and community. Optional: photograph each item with a short caption and create a mini "memory museum" at home.

This honours clothing as connective tissue – stitching us to the people, places, and moments that have shaped us.

Further readings

To deepen your understanding of the themes explored in *The Pursuit of the Power-suit*, consider diving into the following books and resources. Each one offers unique perspectives on the psychology of fashion, self-expression, identity, and empowerment:

"Dress and Identity" by *Mary Ellen Roach-Higgins & Joanne B. Eicher*

A seminal essay on the symbolic role of dress and its link to personal identity.

The Fashioned Body by *Joanne Entwistle*

An exploration of the social and cultural dimensions of the dressed body.

Enclothed Cognition by *Adam & Galinsky (2012)*

The original research study introducing the theory of how clothes influence cognition and behavior.

Positive Psychology: Theory, Research and Applications by *Hefferon & Boniwell*

A comprehensive guide to the science of wellbeing which underpins much of your theoretical framing.

The Social Psychology of Dress by *Susan Kaiser*

A valuable academic reference for those exploring the broader sociocultural context of fashion choices.

Big Dress Energy by *Shakaila Forbes-Bell*

This book helps readers understand how to make more meaningful style choices that support confidence, identity, and wellbeing.

Worn: A People's History of Clothing by *Sofi Thanhauser*

A beautifully researched cultural history exploring how clothes shape economies, identities, and lives across the globe.

You Are What You Wear by *Jennifer Baumgartner*

A closet-deep dive into how our fashion choices reflect our inner world – and how changing our wardrobe can change our life.

Index

www.ingramcontent.com/pod-product-compliance
Lightning Source LLC
Chambersburg PA
CBHW070338270326
41926CB00017B/3914